LIMESTONE

AN EPIC POEM OF BARBADOS

ALSO BY ANTHONY KELLMAN

Poetry

The Black Madonna
In Depths of Burning Light
The Broken Sun
Watercourse
The Long Gap
Wings of a Stranger

Fiction

The Coral Rooms
The Houses of Alphonso

ACKNOWLEDGEMENTS

Grateful acknowledgment is made to the editors of the following publications in which sections of this poem appeared:

Margin: Exploring Modern Magical Realism for Part One, Chapter Six (as "A Diviner's Burial");
Obsidian III (North Carolina) for Part One, Chapter Two, sections three and four (as "Anna Fortuna");
Wasafiri (London) for Chapter Twenty-Five, Part Three (as "Coast");

Chapter Five in Part One appeared in the anthology *Coloring Book,* Ed. Boice-Terrel Allen. Pittsburg, Rattlecat Press, 2004 (as "A Final Battle").
Chapter Twenty-three, section three, appeared in the anthology, *CRUX: A Conversation in Words and Images, South Africa to South USA*. Eds. Alice Lovelace et al., Atlanta: Fulton County Arts Council, 2007 (as "Levinia").

ANTHONY KELLMAN

LIMESTONE

AN EPIC POEM OF BARBADOS

PEEPAL TREE

First published in Great Britain in 2008
Peepal Tree Press Ltd
17 King's Avenue
Leeds LS6 1QS
UK

ISBN 13: 9781845230036

Peepal Tree gratefully acknowledges Arts Council support

PART ONE

CHAPTER ONE

1
Gravely weighing present
time, Ichirouga
eyes the burial mound on Brandon's

beach where, grave and few,
his braves slowly
circle the fires of death; wood of

sorrow wrenching dreams and
pushing darkness
from out its shell; hatred burning

quickly as a roof; faces
kilned with ancient grief.
Spanish invaders had struck last

night with muskets, slaughter.
One hut is used to hold
the women in. Ichirouga

sees one man, all his bulk
clad with lust and salt,
enter the windowless bohio.

Women's screams lift like
crows. The roof and
walls slatted with fronds and gully vines,

shake with the sailor's panting
thrusts. Masked by
the screams, Ichirouga advances.

In the hut virgins' blood
now spots the ground;
oily stench of the sailor's sweat;

choking fumes of liquor;
bulging uncased belly;
breath rank, teeth carious: Ichi-

rouga hacks and thrusts
with spear and club.
Thud of wood on flesh and bone.

Bead of fire from musket,
aimed at him in there,
bluntly cracks in the humid air.

He limps outside with spear
and club of blood.
Women cowering. The sailor dead.

The sky is washed in deep-
est blue. No clouds.
All that brilliance high up there.

His dead are strewn like birds.
The thieves put to sea,
rowed away with his family.

Squinting eyes broke the sun's
wall hanging on
the coast. Slow and wary, his remn-

ant came from hiding,
their spirits dark,
their glory dimmed.

2

Shape of heart was loving
words, easy mastery
of grace and beauty, the twins of charm.

Their genius: harming
no-one. Even small
insects had their cosmic place.

They paddled seas, whole oceans,
dugouts burrowing south,
challenge death in the Dragon's Mouth.

Were they not meant for sky
or for this life?
What killed them? Their doubt? Or war?

One-sided war. The mad-
dened plunge for land,
thirst for gold. They're forced to flee.

Once clans attacked for man-flesh,
weapons, women,
but in their leaving peace returned.

These strangers left them bare
as the eaten
turtle shells that lined hut walls.

Old times rose like misty
seas, salt pricking I-
chirouga's eyes like needles. He

saw the traps the men had
set for shellfish, turtles,
flying fish, shark, and birds for food

and feathers; saw the hammocks'
languid sway and
women's work in field and hut.

He loved their oiled bodies,
perfumed skin fest-
ooned with beads from petals, shells.

He summons dreams of peace
in the falling arc
of the machineel's blistered leaf

and the sparrow's wheel, wants
nothing but to hold the
ancient ways from Behring to Guiana.

Poised as a ceramic bird,
his fragile moment's
full with fish and pots. Bites at Shroud,

Laycock and Jones, Chandler,
pots all brimming good.
Steep the jagged cliff face, breakers

in the air, brief respite
from the shadow of fear.
Lower lands again open for trade:

fish for maize, potato,
long cassava shoots
at Mapp's Cave, Three Houses, Luke.

But unmatched wars have brought
him to this thought:
Here hunters have no enduring

place, nowhere to run from
stronger enemies –
inland rivers few and far between;

no protected coast;
nothing but coconuts
and lines of scattered mangroves.

Broken head-of-wind clan
carrying its bows
sees his lines of sorrow ripple

the shallows quick as
pollinating arrows.
Has the wind betrayed its clan,

bringing coarse-bearded men
in linen blankets
scowling across the ocean?

They'd eat a catch of conch
and whelks. Made strong,
morning'd bring them across the sea's

rough love and silver light.
So desperate canoes
needle northward two by two,

the early morning mist
now risen like a ghost.
Dominica may bring more luck.

CHAPTER TWO

1
Now lost from human hands,
the island waits,
faintly choralling breath a hiss

of surf. This rest, this pause,
restores to soil its
virgin vigour, tempts lustful eyes.

Calling fellow Britons,
riff-raff feeding on air,
John Powell urges them to sail with him.

Soil and climate
favoured settlement in
this crown of all the Caribbees.

Seat for war, great mart, trade
would flourish with
the rising sun.

In silky shirt and fierce
light-headed joy,
John Powell nods, and then each William

Courteen boy shins up the
rigging to unfurl
the westward bowing sails.

Crossing their ocean path
a Dutch slave trader comes,
bound for Brazil, full-rigged, wanton,

priapic as an arching
dolphin. Raucous laughter
rings at the sight of splashing hull.

The two ships slow, unsure.
A fight or truce? John Powell
ignores the feud at least today.

The captains bargain. Dutch-
man pays eight Blacks
for English food supplies.

2
Nameless, eyes fixed on
the horizon, stares far
beyond to where his country lay.

They thought he'd gone insane,
his gaze unblinking,
jaw set, his skin like darkest coal.

Trip's end saw men and hogs
stretch thankfully,
cramped from thirty-five days at sea.

A fort was built, a flag
run up. They carved
their names deep on a fustic tree.

Banyans, mythic giants,
bearded, kept watch,
gateway gods, each air root a latch.

Nameless first thought his capture
would be as back at home:
slaves treated as one of household,

where skill could lift
like royal palms,
crown with success the man who

loyally worked. Only one goal
could never be reached.
Slaveman couldn't become a king.

Here they saw him as less
than a man. Their tone
sliced him deeper than knives,

though he didn't understand
their words. Cuffs and
heavy hands forced down his head.

Whiplash followed; speech to
pale man cut short.
Soon, he grasped those enforced names:

'master', 'mistress', learnt to
swiftly lower eyes,
shoulders, clasp hands to make address.

The English words, fired
like bullets in his ears,
pry hard at his native tongue.

3.
Soon other settlers came,
threshing on the blue,
gambling to renew their fortunes.

Then land disputes arose
'til finally, they all
locked fists and began a brawl.

This Carlisle won with great
tobaccoed weight, supporters
made merry with freehold reward.

Wealth that had been bruised,
grew strong again, rooting
the pattern of white dominance.

At first the land was mostly
tilled for smoke.
Cotton, indigo, followed suit,

craving labour. Caribs
had long departed from the isle,
trade in Blacks was not yet organised.

Poor white labour saved the
day: a baser sort:
refugees, indentured Scots,

convicts, rogues and Irish
riff-raff, volunteer serfs
to serve the planter's ceaseless need.

Slaves, yet not slaves – bondage
fixed for a term then ended.
(Nameless saw his own bondage lengthen.)

Whites who showed some industry,
some zeal, could rise
as artisans, overseers, ledger clerks.

Some, in time, bought land and
slaves with savings eked
from jobs like these.

15

But Nameless witnesses
other whites as shabbily
dressed as he. Sees three women, seven

grown men sharing one mud
hut, their children in rags,
dirt-soiled, racing in play

in the cracked slave yard. Sees
men with raw red legs,
seared by the sun, still wear the kilts

in which they came, the wind
rapping their tattered loins,
their skins sun dried and peeling.

Others, seen from time to
time, were worse than these,
living like bats in nearby caves.

Nameless left the yard to
find the cotton field,
went past the teeming duck pond,

past the royal palms, his
fronded favourites,
cannonball, and mahogany.

Morning mist had lifted.
He stares towards the far
horizon, still dreaming of home.

Sketchy fading visions.
Blurry faces on a track.
Slanting, endless, falling rain.

Clanging iron shackles.
Deepest forest night.
Darkest hold where airlessness and stink

stifled for days. There was
a woman who drew
lines across her burnished face.

Who she was he didn't
know, could not recall.
Something stirred in his mind and fell

unformed. His mother? Wife?
He tries to name
those of his closest kin.

His own name went blank.
Just waves, the low coffin,
stench of shit and sweat.

But now Nameless sees more
of his kind arrive as
cotton gives way to spikes of cane.

Sugar along with sun
and rain, needed the kind
of hands able to take this heat.

4.
Now, as dawn spread out its
sad, deep-tortured smile, and
Downing cried: 'What a virgin isle!'

English titles flowed on
prominent manjacks,
Thomas Modyford and James Drax –

dear-bought rewards from the
soon to be headless Charles,
then from republican Cromwell.

Smaller estates swarmed and
merged with larger ones,
forming alliances that scythed the land –

Royalists scorning Roundheads.
Parliament, though, soon brought
all sides to heel and chartered them:

Mermaid Tavern held the
truce and Cromwell's men gave
land-rights with low levies as white-

skin Bajans took control
of the state. A white flag,
boat-borne, flapped into Royal bay.

5.
Slaves increased like cow grass,
trapped in fields of pain,
their shoulders scarred from loads of cane.

They shuffle dully, all
hope seared away,
weeding-gang faces sucked in with want:

boys and girls and pregnant
women, the very old
and convalescing folks,

feet barnacled in dust,
heads padded with grief.
crocus-sack clothes to hold the grime.

By now the slave Nameless
was called Simon.
Every morning at six, he slings

cane bill over shoulder,
sets off for the fields,
or takes his place in the lane of rags

plodding onwards towards
the Great House. Simon was
regal but ragged, a royal palm

whose bark, like scales,
was flaking. Wails,
hollers, sad ballads ease the strain.

At dusk they take the same
mud-tracks for home,
walking slower, still humming tunes.

Simon, haggard, reaches
his cabin made of dried
mud, then turns to his friends and waves.

Night comes on with croaking
frogs and night-birds' calls,
stray-dog sounds in the echoing hills.

Inside, a woman stokes
the fire. Four stones
ring the flames that lick hard beneath

an earthen pot. He loved
her well. Swollen stomach,
the fruit of master's coarse order:

'Breed!' Yet even at this
late, close to the earth,
brooding maternal stage, daily

labour called her early
to the sunbaked fields,
weeding, hoeing between the canes.

6.
'A dangerous kind of brute,'
the planters ruled. They
tighten slave codes to tame the dark

beasts by brandings, whippings,
slitting noses, severing
limbs and iron bit to seal the mouth.

Simon had fled one night,
plunged through sugar-cane,
mauve and arrowed, sticky with juice,

demeanour a black crow's
wing on soft satin,
terror quickening his strides. Eyes

pierce the darkness. Sweat rushes
from him as he speeds,
cane-fronds razoring his arms, his

legs. The canopied woods
hear his cries, dogs' yelps,
see the lights reflected on his

naked, captured form. Eyes
shut, inner sense projects
a speeding rush of images:

of dodging the planters'
shining black broughams slow-
wheeling to town; of the rum-fumed

smell of Bridgetown's Roebuck
Tavern, beckoning with
its whores; of the malodorous

river draining two parishes,
dull like the eyes of a
pox-wracked planter; of the wharf's stale

nauseous smell of pigtails,
pork, salt-fish, molasses,
hanging over the city streets;

of soft, blue-veined hands, white
on his ebony skin,
country English voice telling him:

Such fine timbers, Simon.
What manhood you have.
Palm-tree Negro, my wild sweet Black.

When house-slave Joey saw
all this with telltale eyes,
witness to Simon's lengthy stays,

one ear pressed to the door,
for moaning, rustling proof,
Simon knew his life was gone.

He hears trees rustling madly:
curious monkeys
making riot in mangrove leaves.

They tie rope round his hands
and hoist him up.
The clearing is wide, washed in moon-

light, frogs' objections,
night-birds' warbles, and the sour
excitement of a lynch-mobs' smell.

Involuntary piss
froths from Simon, mixing
with the sweat that soaks the ground.

He tries to plant his feet
in the earth to stop his doom.
But a snorting, drumming horse pulls

up sweat-lathered and a
a bowler hat dismounts.
Simon hears the sound of buckled boots

approach, and squints through the
blinding lanterns' glare thrust
in his face. "Master…," without hope

he cries. "Simon, confess
your sordid sin so God
may pardon you, you heathen brute!"

"Face your judgment!" Face still
hot with rum, he nods
and two men tear off Simon's shirt,

rough-rope him to the pole.
Massa unwraps a whip
with tip of bone. Thirty-five of

one hundred strokes he gives,
each lash a frond of pain,
until Simon falls unconscious.

He's revived with smelling salts,
then John, with pail in hand,
takes crushed hot peppers and rubs them

in his wounds. Massa calls
for a knife and, cold as ice,
rips down Simon's ragged pants.

In one swift move, the knife
connects; Simon's manhood
writhes on the ground. Massa steps back,

his laugh dry as starch, calls
one of his men to chop
off one of the runaways feet.

Blood and more blood washes
the age; for days the sad
slaves roam about, praying each drop

will put a curse on Massa's
young. With glazed austere
appearances, their silence slices

the sad hours – going slow,
skimping work, spoiling food –
once, with ground glass's burning rod.

Grief for Simon, slave just
turned thirty-seven,
slave who would never see his son.

He lingers to the eve
of locusts that ruin crops;
eve of fire that darkens the city;

eve of gusts that fell the
fustic tree on whose bark
the first settlers carved their names;

eve of drought's ruin, when
walls of great houses cracked.
Signs and wonders, but no penitence.

Slowly, life returns to
spent, bruised frames, locked in
the rhythms of illusive pastoral.

See those sable Susannah's
in fetching dishabille,
down by the river scrubbing sheets,

bleaching-bushes strewn with
clothes. But see the watching
elders startle when a gust of wind

catches in the hanging
linen, booms and cracks with
the sound of rebellious guns.

Little wonder planters'
houses were small forts,
cisterns to damp the fire of slaves.

Little wonder crises
panicked them to search
slaves' huts for evidence of arms –

the sergeants inching inside
their silent fears, under
the secret glances of Ga, Igbo,

Fanti, Ewe, Edo,
Dahomey, Andangme,
Yoruba and Ashanti...

secret glances gleaming
with rage as when a light
flickers over polished ebony.

7.
Dusk, and only the braying
donkeys tied to the cala-
bash trees disturb plantation peace,

when Anna Fortuna
in handmade, flowing, flour-
sack skirt that writhes with her easy strides;

when Anna Fortuna,
loyal house-slave who, each
day, coyly plaits her mistress's hair;

when Anna Fortuna,
dung-basket on her arm,
slides by Cuffee's small hut where four

men and women chat
intensely outside.
Crop was over and slaves with rare

easy laughter enjoyed
looser hours when men
straddled high drums and women's hems

lifted over legs that
shone with oil from hogs'
lard. Then Anna's keen ear over-

hears the Igbo Cuffee
say: 'We wait too long,
but now is time for blood for blood.'

Anna wasn't sure she'd
heard the first part right,
but 'Blood for blood,' she repeats twice.

Hurrying to Mistress
who's sipping Sunday tea,
she spills all she heard. Mistress falls

off her chair. The floral
china cup's handle
breaks, and tea soaks the whole table.

Within hours the lawmen
swarm into the slaves'
quarters. Huddled in corners, arms

wrapped around their children,
women crouch and wail.
Blood-eyed men are shoved at gunpoint

into the open yard,
then questioned, jailed.
Next day, trials begin. One soul,

under torture, tells of
plans to raise a revolt
on each estate across the island,

and slit their masters' throats.
They'd fire the canes with
guava rods tipped with oil and lit.

Slaves would seize the island.
Cuffee, the acclaimed
elder, would be their shining king....

Six were burnt alive and
eleven had heads
chopped off. Seventeen razed with lead.

Three hung. They stand, these last,
noosed stiffly on a cart,
The horse, once nudged, then walks away.

Then sudden smell of shit,
bulging eyes and twisted
mouth. Where once the smell of roses,

now the stench of burning
flesh and the beady-eyed
crows soaring in the smoke-hazed sky.

Anna Fortuna was
the toast of Barbados,
freed as model obedient servant.

8.
A storm was scything hard
towards the island, but
planters' merriment was rumming high

in talk of triumph over
heathens' treacherous blood-
thirsty midnight plans to slay them all;

in talk of Hall's man slave
who tried to abort the plot
for love of his own master's life;

how his fellows threatened
and fearing for his life,
Hall's man ran but returned next night;

how that happy night, through
Good Providence, hand-
maid Anna heard him talking low

to fellow countrymen;
how Mistress was soon primed,
and under threat of life Hall's slave

confessed. 'God bless the Cap-
tains who pressed those rats.'
'Brutes! They won't try again, I hope to God.'

'Our force much stricter now.'
'Anna!' 'Massa Gov'nor!'
'Thanks to God, for his mercy endures.'

Now trees rock and judder
as the hurricane whips in,
and rivers swell and rise in flood.

Less than twenty houses on
Hall's still stand at midnight.
The threat of death's the leveller,

as slaves, overseers, masters
crowd the cellar of the House.
Wind and rain, now in battling clutch,

rap and slay the tallest
calabash trees
that crash like wildest castanets.

Anna alone in her
wooden cabin, her reward,
fears it won't withstand the storm.

Glances, deer-like, towards
the Great House, hesitates,
until wind's buffets make her run.

Anna Fortuna, caught
in the middle, never saw
the huge joist rise from the wood shed,

lift and surf on the wind
like a spear's swift dance
towards her too-slow turning head.

Mercy comes swiftly as
she falls, free yet slave still,
exiled by each world. Lost soul.

9.
Christmas comes and Massa
slackens a few rules.
Rivers gurgle like fed babies.

Slaves have fattened pigs to
kill, then cure with bay rum
leaves and the acid juice of limes.

A calabash's measured blood
from necks' bright flood
caught from that fountain. Set it down,

cure, then mix with grated
seasoned potato.
Fill the innards: rich black pudding.

Gyrate, amuse your boss.
'Looka! The massa
take Aura as a partner to dance!'

'Let them beat their drums. Such
crude imitations...
poorest sketch of our marching bands.'

10.
The island weak from war,
Sampson, a restless slave,
whispers in other ready ears

slow burning for freedom:
watchman Ben John, ranger
Hammon, other trusted artisans.

On a mud floor, by the
downside-up barrel table,
after they'd eaten their fill

of pork and rice and black-
eyed peas, the hand-carved
spoons are placed in the calabash

bowls. A royal palm tree's
rustle hides their voices.
Men press in for Sampson's say.

Trusted, big in name, but
bigger than the name
inside the heart where true strength reigns,

he raised a plan that winged
each mind with dreams
large as freedom and its rewards.

First seize the master's house
and horse. Then hold
Bridgetown's forts, its guns, its swords;

crush the Gov'nor, soldiers,
every peril,
free all slaves from the Bridgetown goal.

They eyed the right moment,
just as Cuffee'd done,
to take the early advantage.

Twice, arriving British
fleets would force retreat,
postpone their locked-up energies.

The change of dates confused
some of Cuffee's men.
Blunders followed and then arrests.

Informing on Ben John,
how he'd seemed on edge,
house slave Faustus took his silver,

betrayed his fellows with
a poisoned kiss, sent
ninety-two men to cruel deaths.

CHAPTER THREE

1.
Years roll by the changeless
grace of green cane fronds,
turning windmills, axles' groan

down the shaded cart roads
lined with labourers;
breadfruit's certainty, haggard hours;

sunrise's sighs lit with
wings of the sparrow
and the slave's deep natural sorrow;

bush tea brewed, cornbread baked
for those bidden to the fields,
shoulders slung with sharp cutlasses;

great house gardens bleeding
poinsettia's lake of blood;
'U' carts heaped with canes; the yard's lines

gathering; incessant
rumbling of the sugar mill's
machines;

stray chicks vainly picking
at spots where sugar clumps
spilled and stuck in the yard's thick dust;

arcing cranes ascending
their pentatonic scales
over stalks and the crushing rollers;

night falling; fires stoked,
women fussing, jesting
gayly, dresses hoisted above

their knees; grimy children
still out playing in
the drought-bare yard; in the gloom

cane arrows rise and fan
the air, stretching beyond
green hills, cabins, the masters' marked

graveyards, the slaves' unmarked
within each village:
death in life and each life in death.

2.
Sunday morning. Slaves keep
church in their own way.
Restless children don't wait to play.

A boy with Coroman-
tee glistening skin,
pulses naked around the yard

where sun-clad cocks and hens
with scratching feet
rake out worms and insect morsels.

Cackling gladly, other
children join the dance.
Dust rises and falls, gently drifting

over the yard. Haloed
by sun, motes spark brightly,
starry walls in a glint of faith.

Some boys approach this new
one to know his name.
'Bussa,' he says and speeds along,

proud. His hand is holding
nuts, thumb-sized, ovular,
yellow, blemished where they were touched

with small insect-brown spots.
Says he, 'Dum is lots
hang 'pon tree underneath de hill.'

The curious youths sur-
round the boy who, teasing,
conceals the treasures in his hand.

'Kola nuts,' says Bussa,
startled, as his mind's
limbo murmurs, and images

seethe like grains of sifting sand.
Too young to remember
well, he struggles hard to net what's

swarming in his mind. 'Father...
uncles... in my hut
long time back....' He then bites the nut,

recoils and spits and reels.
He doesn't taste the sting-
ing sharpness, feel the rush of energy

that loosed his father's mouth,
made self sprout large, and talk
keep up his kinfolk through the night.

The tangy pungent pod
he'd tasted once, had made
him run for water from the well.

This fruit was sweet. Its firm
pulp didn't turn bright orange,
release its pungency when bitten on.

Nor could it be bitten
right through. When his teeth
met the hardness, he'd gagged in grief,

spat out the half-chewed nut,
stared at its imposture,
with questioning loss-filled eyes.

The others laughed and one
said, 'They's almonds.
Hard hard shell with a good sweet nut

down inside. Is only
de inside we does eat.
Knock off outside and tek de nut.

Leh me show you.' Taking
the nuts from the new boy,
finding a rock near a rose-head bush,

his teacher stooped and turned
a fruit so it was propped
straight on its seam, then, grinning, knocked

the outer skin until
he reached the inner shell.
Smiling proudly, he cracked the shell,

took the brown kernel out,
broke it, put half in mouth,
said 'Ummm' twice and then dared Bussa

to eat the other half.
And all them laugh,
wanting some too. So Bussa led

them along a track, up
a hill's grass lip
under which the wide almond stood.

Instinct will push against
one's long-lost ghosts:
seething grains of thought: of ships,

stink and bloody, holding
cargoes of dry bones.
Bussa knew and he didn't know.

Knew what? Knew the feeling –
heavy as manacles –
of dread at the blankness of mind-

deranging fits; knew the
stories, half believed, for
the teller forgot whole scenes, and

pained in telling, would sweat
like young Bussa in night's
long wrestle, showing that all he'd

sensed, though seeming real,
had no clear proof. Was that
woman really his mother? When

he heard talk of this land,
distant, all-black, something
stirred deep in him, something unknow-

able, unreachable,
a cradling dawn,
a life, it seemed, that had no end.

So, in this ripe almond
season, Bussa felt both
pain and joy to see, now sharp, now

fading, a past that shone
through light slanting showers,
wondering if that rainbow led

to Wari's sacred cotton-
tree where the spirits,
childlike, wait to be brought to life,

and women wanting children
sit hopeful every day,
patient, wearing its gown of shade.

3.
A rebel age creeps past.
Discreet, the older slaves
whisper of Cuffee whose memory

still inspires their dreams,
though lawmen, everywhere
hard and harsh, arrest that name,

keep it locked up under
whiplash, like the gun-
barking laws made to hush the drum.

Sugar's sticky web trapped
all on the island,
yet Massa clung to his English

ways: profit, class and skin.
But for all their wealth,
trips to England, and strutting pomp,

Bajan whites, to English-
borns, were but mimicking
parrots stuck in a cage of trash,

dressed in finest English
wool in the sun-struck
tropics; fat with wealth's arrogance,

uncultured, blank and with
no spark of finer feeling,
knowing only of ledgers, talk

of threatened slave revolts
in teacups' steam of doubt;
attic's pile of London clothes and guns.

The other class of Whites,
history's tattered kilt:
peasants, vagrants, wage labourers,

servitude's own children,
stranded with no social song.
For most it was a life of scratching

and patching, sugar-sack
clothing, eating slave food,
hooking jacks to eat or breeding chickens.

Wrenched with sorrow at the
hovelled lives of kin,
Steele campaigned for jobs for them;

anything to end the shame,
their begging and the pain.
Steele lost. Nothing changed. Their will

to work leaked out, so
Poyer cried that now the
'Negroes' lot is better than Whites!'

Yet mobile through their skin,
after bondage ended,
some left the past to make great gain.

One day, as sun's thread
stitched sky's blue bed,
faintly first, then with intenser hue,

Bussa eyes one such man
whose military strides
carry echoes of past hard times,

those days of hookworm and
inbreeding public shame,
lodgings worse than the slave's mud hut.

This man had found, at Bayley's,
the means to make a life
of tolerable and stable clime:

a skirt of land, a wife
who'd walk long miles to change
their garden produce for fine goods

from France, her huckster skills
learnt well from slaves –
whom she despised, frowned at each day.

Bussa winces. The man
stamps briskly through the yard,
muddy boots like sows messing up

the floor. The chickens
scamper, like the thoughts
slaves have wondering who'll be next

to feel the overseer's boot,
the biting, burning whip,
the twisting, dangling, strangling rope.

Bussa never winced a-
gain. He was thirty-five
when he steadied his head, his nerve,

stared the officer down,
made him blink and look away.
Bussa would never bend again.

These lowest ranks of whites
were squalid as their sties.
Rablands, parched by the sun, their lot.

Bussa watches all: sees
how most, those born right here,
become a new Creole being.

Those born, like him, in Africa
were feared as threats, treated
more harshly to put out their flame.

Once, at Grand Crop Over,
Bussa watches some slaves
faking accent, posture, dancing

quadrille and gavotte,
on day of jubilee,
sycophant, he thinks, to Europe's ways,

But thought of origins
would sometimes nudge Creoles,
and Bussa takes their questions,

advises on rites of birth
and death, meanings of
words and music kept underground.

Bussa groups the slaves by
tribe, secretly teaches them
dance and song for next jubilee.

There, drummers crouch across
each palm-trunk drum's curved back,
beat the goatskin with discovered

fire, while other youths
each armed with a long stick,
beat drums' long wooden sides.

Fiddle? None. Nor fipple
flute, nor Scottish fife.
Plenty drum, though, with skins that slice

the night, chilling the dreams
of snoring overseer,
sodden with drinking, song and dance

that Day of Jubilee,
that day when passion,
deep and black, marked the pounding drum.

CHAPTER FOUR

1.
Bussa catches a glimpse
of Nanny with her clothes-
pile near Simmon's unscreened back porch

behind which stood a grove:
guava, mango,
sapodillas and star-apples,

golden apples, pawpaws.
Slaves went to the back door,
straight past evergreen's massive trunk

and leaves that screened the front's
low shrubs, its beds.
Black to back, the unwritten law.

Thick and braided her hair
coiled with enough spring and
reach to grabble all Africa;

her skin was smooth as syrup,
silk-soft in light.
Patience crowned her with easy smiles.

Head-tied, she wears a dress
made of old discarded
dresses. Cherry blossoms stir like sprats.

He'd walked from Bayley's – head
ranger's trusted task to
deliver massa's messages.

He asks, 'De Massa here?'
Nanny only stares.
When he adds a 'Mornin',' she blinks,

straightens, bare feet planted
firmly on the ground.
Nanny stares once more, asks: 'What?'

'You have some letta fo'
him? Let me see it, man.'
She looks it through, then gives it back.

He'd sensed some wisdom as
she'd felt him out with subtle
nuanced gaze. Now this. She'd read

his massa's letter. Here
were depths of silence
layered deep inside her stone.

Silence. Cunning. Bussa
wanted what she had:
secret knowledge of massa's mind.

How could a single word,
one act, so soon expose
promise reaching across an age?

He couldn't say. He knew
what he must do.
Skill was needed, the skill to read.

'You teach me read o' how
we mekking out?
How we fare on de udder isles?

Dey accept Massa slav'ry
same way dat we do?'
'Fight them, shite them wid black arm fight,'

she said. 'But slow, but slow...
You massa black cloud?'
Eyeing Bussa frame north and south,

she smiles: 'I teach yuh try
to read and write.
Teach yuh Toussaint L'Overture.'

'Dis ent no place to hide
a sea-lock soul,' she says.
'Catch we quick in no time at-all.

We got to use up here.'
And with blunt forefinger,
like stabbing beak she probes her hair.

Bussa smiles. His mind is
soaring like a sea crane,
heart's string tugged by her strength and pride.

So Bussa's 'errands' grew,
to steal some precious time,
to pluck the fruits of Nanny's knowing.

Bussa asked of Massa's
life. She told of tables
groaning with flesh of beast and fowl;

cellar's full stock of yams,
eddoes, other roots; the horses
in the coach-house more comfortable

than slave huts; crammed wood store;
arched entries to halls;
floors of marble in dazzling squares;

the airy sitting room,
kitchen and breakfast rooms.
Behind – an exclamation mark –

the stairwell rising to
five bedrooms like tombs
flaunting canopied cordia beds.

'Talk more 'bout their bidness,
their land, properties and
market in slaves,' Bussa requests.

Nanny plays the Mistress
who would, she informs,
simply echo the Massa's tone:

'Bought today at market,
a costly Negro wench,
sound in body and sound in mind

for work in field and house;
Annie, a good plain cook,
a high brown yellow lab'ring wench,

sound as a dollar, genteel,
mannerly and tractable
in spirit and suited well for

work as a house servant.
She's worth the price.
See! The wench is in prime of life!'

Tells Bussa how they talked
of a son who grieved his
father; children's struggles with school work.

How fear of France and Spain
had fled after Lord Nelson's
glorious Trafalgar victory,

but dread of slave revolt
ever worries their minds.
Toussaint's ghost still an angry wind.

Nanny muses, 'I saw
the mistress' soft hand-sown
knickers split by she nou-nou. Then

I know dat's how they sex
wid-out she tek off she
clothes. Dese whites. Dey real mad. Real mad.'

They laugh at this, these two,
and know a true comfort
in mirth. So Nanny invites him

Sunday after church for
food at her small hut.
Bussa says yes and tips his hat.

2.
Bussa watches the broughams,
buggies, gigs rolling
gently over the countryside,

past sugar mills and great
houses, arrowing cane fields
ringed with razoring khus-khus grass;

past horsebacked, musket-wielding
constables, with hounds
baying viciously at their heels;

past a mock English church
built of new-sawn limestone.
Found the village Nanny called home,

her hut half hidden by
a wooden trellis screen white-
specked with fungus, its missing slats

confessing a great house
discard, passion-fruit vines
gripping the frames. Peppery smell

of tomato plants in
full ripening assaults
Bussa close by Nanny's door.

He pauses, reaches out.
Sleek red fruit in one hand,
with the other he knocks. The door

is opened. Talk of ranger
duties – maintaining bound-
aries, paths and animal pens;

cleaning buggies, gigs and
polishing broughams;
mending horse shoes and bullock carts.

'Wha' I do? I wake-up
children, help them wash and
dress. I clean and keep the house fresh.

Dey children loves to read
dey books. I learn
read too.' Laid on a pillow filled

with sour grass, a quilt, half-
made, tells him Mistress taught
her all the arts of needle work.

'Tries to keep she daughters'
fingers always busy.
Hard thing.' Pointing to some baskets,

Nanny says, 'I make them
for carry Massa's dung.
I fetch it and I cure de vines.'

They talk and laugh and eat
full plates of peas and rice,
chicken, pig's tail, and plantain pie,

this day when coal-pots steam
with life and the cala-
bash bowls all hold the strength of song,

when cool clear water from
the monkey pot tastes –
poured by Nanny – like the finest wine.

Nanny's hut becomes their
refuge. There he learns of
Toussaint; there he learns to read and write.

3.
Roused by Haiti's blazing
story, his spirit soon
comes boldly leaping in a flame.

Bussa studies local
forces: the array of
power stacked on the planters' side:

frequent army visits,
well-armed regiments,
soldier tenants and naval fleets;

expansive net of roads;
track of redcoat soldiers'
boots, marching over hill and vale;

forts with stockpiles mottling
the windy, salt-swept coasts.
Bussa weighs this soberly; sees

planters crazed with power,
church teaching obedience,
token bribes for discontented slaves.

Most slaves were Creoles now,
Africa a distant story.
Could they be aroused to fight?

Self's own manumission
was the dream, preferred to
freedom for all if it meant armed attack.

Bussa knew the planters'
strategies to win slaves'
compliance: the door to one's own

sexual partner, mothers
keeping home their children,
easier travel, a plot of land.

In time, the thought of change
to risk these modest gains
turns rebel blood, it seems, to water.

Was it that now they felt
a deeper sense of place?
Offspring tending the fathers' graves?

Why did they yell in fear,
'Massa, please don't send dis
slave to neighbouring sulphur isles!'?

Whatever the reason
is dead-season now. What's
certain? The rebel spirit slept.

For while some other islands
struggled still, the price
of freedom furrows limestone brows.

'All we could do's run 'way,'
Nanny says with a sneer
to him, 'and forfeit all we pride.'

But Bussa holds to his
vision of a time when words,
boldly weaponed with thought and skill,

become the blade to bring
the managers to bargain-
ing's mutual resolution.

Bold words should be tried,
he says, before they go
to war. So towards the great house,

united in doubtful hope,
they march till their sweat falls
on Bayley's sun-struck steps.

They knock and wait.
Wordless, contemptuous,
Massa Bayley caresses his gun.

They walk some fifteen miles
to town to raise a point
of law, and late that night, feelings

swollen like a raging
sea, the estate lawyer
makes them wait, until imperious

behind his desk he lets
them voice their ancient
grievances. They'd heard that England's

parliament had banned the trade
in slaves, but that their island
masters refused to set them free.

Their ignorance mocked,
reminded of their duties
the lawyer sends them back to work.

They grieve that coloured men
believe that their own
black mothers should not be freed.

CHAPTER FIVE

Myself, Bussa, witness
the breeding of the slaves.
Younger men were chosen. Each day,

I thank god for keeping
shame from me own self.
Yet, it hurt me to hear the cries,

Creole and African –
me own dying kind –
grating and threshing my spirit.

Ripening girls were given
money, best rations, work-
loads light as thistle's touch to breed

like cattle. It grieve me
heart to see we makin
pickney self for Massa's profit.

But she who taught me how
to read and write, who make
me welcome in she wooden hut –

our love had stretched deep down,
like when yams send dey roots
spreading steady inside green fields

to fill a man with joy
and hope and, in his dreams,
he brings his harvest to his bride.

But Fate must have us go
to war; loving had to
wait until we'd quenched our thirst for

freedom. The day we'd heard
the Trade had died, we danced
and sang; blackest rivers ran through

our veins. Nanny had said
'We only goal is tuh be free.
Freedom's redeemed with sacrifice

and sweat of mothers, fathers,
children: all our sweat
running together like a flood.'

On me each eye was pinned.
I was mature in years
but vigorous still. Some knew me

as a man who knew the
crafts of war. Others respect
me for my rank as ranger.

On other estates slaves
were watching for the glow
of fired cane-trash over Bayley's

brow, signal of war; to
each the orange flames the
fuse to light the torch of freedom.

Heaven's darkness cloaked our
skins in well-matched tones,
our bodies taut as love-vines on walls.

Massa, mistress, children,
well dinnered, snore deep,
would not be roused – fed on a dish

seasoned with patience,
peppered with resentment
to disguise the sleeping herbs.

Nanny stays home under
pretence of a sore throat,
head leaf-wrapped, just to play the part.

Under night-borne cover,
crouched in the tension-thick
silence, torches in hand, we light

the future of our isle,
thinking awhile:
Burn them houses on Monday; make

them shout for water's balm.
On Tuesday, burn the canes,
make them bawl in fear again.

Murder whitemen Wednesday,
make them cry for mercy,
make Massa's houses run with blood.

Our snake-soft hisses sound
like wind moving through grass.
Penned horses wouldn't even neigh.

Our unity was tight
as braided hair.
Rebel units in readiness

waited to move on main
estates across the isle,
each led by its trusted headman.

Jackey, leading driver
over at Simmon's
kept our units as one.

With help from John Ranger,
Jackey, inspired, moves
round each unit and takes them words

of hope. With hands held firm
each one prays in turn,
asking God to assist our quest.

They divide up the rice
and pork the women cooked
with love that morning. All eat and sing,

resigned to fate, and, strong
in spirit, fix their thoughts
on Monday and what must be done.

We raid each boiler house
for pitchforks, axes,
gather guava sticks tipped with oil.

Surrounded by frogs and
crickets, with our hands
clenched in anger, we strike as planned

with knives, machetes, and fire.
One quarter of the fields
burning bright, so sweet a fragrance.

But kettle drum sounds came
with breaking light over
the dewy grass, the harbinger

of war. Red uniforms.
A sounding conch and a
militiaman falls and more whites

stumble to their knees on
the ground. But I knew they'd
send signals quickly for more troops.

Tuesday, remnant slaves all
gather at Bayley's.
Death or glory, capture never.

We fought them there and fought
at Golden Grove,
dripping centuries' sweat, our grief.

Bayley's reeked with the stench
of death and the blood,
mostly ours, lay in spreading pools.

Firearms cracked the air and
swords hissed, mingling steel with
the flesh of those who would not be slaves.

But our machetes and knives
were slicing at the chains:
Europe's 'gift' to our freeborn race.

Massa joins the war – the
mistress weeping on the
porch, clutching hold of his shirt-tail.

Massa looms with horse and
gun but my soul lifts me
up to drag him from his saddle.

We strike the ground as one,
our blood, sweat and spit
merging in the swirling dust.

My fists rise and fall in
great tidal hollers of
rage, but we are now one at last.

My blood-smeared blade rears up
to stab his heart,
fear like spiders covering his face.

His bulging eyes are veined
with hate; I know he hoped
that God would chop him down and it

would not be some Black closing
his life's gate. Then a shot
rings out and blood spreads in my head

until the world goes dark.
Death came fast, as I led
our troops in the St. Phillip's heat.

Great ancestors saw my
captors' sunless hearts
and saw my spirit's restlessness.

Good souls they bore me up
and set my spirit free
to wing its journey home.

CHAPTER SIX

Over heaving broad-backed
water with its reef-bones
that clatter with my people's grief,

ancient wings, with widest
threshing urgency
mount in dazzling immensity

April's washed blue sky –
these flashing crows' wings
contoured by glints of light:

spirit's duty. Nestled
safely on ancestral wings,
sad, yet joyed to be going home,

looking back, I see them
hoist me on a cart,
raise Massa from the dust and dirt,

dangling, bloody. Soldiers
carry him carefully
towards the Great House. Mistress rushes

out to meet them, her white
cotton nightgown whirling
in haste, frills lapped in dirt and blood.

One son, hesitant in the
doorway, weeps and wails.
Proving manhood, the elder marches

father-ward to aid them
slowly up the steps.
Cane fronds wave as the 'U' cart leaves,

cartwheels groaning to reach
the clearing. Even though
dead a' ready, they hoist me over

the biggest cannon's mouth
and douse me with oil.
Fired flesh drops off in cindered chunks.

My head remains in place.
One raises his sword,
and severs it.

With scorn, he takes it up.
They find my hut,
raise the skull on a bamboo stake

for all the crows to view.
My spirit grows heavy,
but beating ancestral wings bear

the weight of my sorrow –
an undertow sighing,
breaking like the water below.

As distance grows my view
is hazier, but I glimpse
Nanny holding my skull. She wraps

it slow with a piece of
old crocus like pone
draped with banana leaves, brings

it to the yard. The tribe
begins to swell: old men
women, children; Creole, African.

I swell again with grief,
but song's relief
reaches me, joyous and sad. The bird

of spirit holds me close
as we soar over the
lamenting ocean's sighing breast.

Laments, chants, prayers
rise triumphant
over reefs of ancestral bone.

Nanny's hands then calmly
lower my remains
into the grave. Women whose names

mean good hope and courage
sustain her with song,
adding strength to her earth-borne groans.

Beads that journey'd over
coasts in Africa, big
carnelian stars, are passed from hand

to hand. Cowry chains of
dogs' teeth, fish vertebrae,
are passed with due solemnity.

Beads of local flora,
copper bracelet and
copper ring; a metal blackbird;

next, my iron knife, my
old beloved clay pipe
fired to buff with a brownish stem,

polished smooth, no seam to
show the moulding; kaolin
for new ones; tobacco, cloth, mats,

pots and bowls of food, all
needed for my journey,
watched by the spirits who bear me up.

So Nanny helps persuade
the ancestors to hug
my soul, though my body

will never feel the hold
of native soil.
With love more constant than death,

Nanny takes each object
with such calm faith, knowing
these gifts will all be brought to me

in time's perfection.
With a crane's benign
and careful grace, she arcs her hand

and places these supplies
with my remains,
gently, just where they ought to be.

PART TWO

CHAPTER SEVEN

1.
In 1838 the last chain link snaps;
the planters scowl, then, think perhaps
it's an advantage not to care
for their slaves' food or health, and where
self-serving kindness fitfully held place,
planters' now show their truest face:
a hobble thrust in freedom's course
made without one morsel of remorse,
fulfilling with draconian
fist, their divine right since time began.
New order is the same old one,
made to thwart Black folks' freedom run.
Token coloured ownerships
of land and city businesses –
nowhere enough for equity.
For sure they'll purge the heresy
of black desire; the insolence to shirk
their destiny of endless canefield work.

When fervent voices urge their dream,
the planters quote the 'bible' theme
of duty – out of context: 'Accept Ham's curse,
your lot's to be a docile labour force.'
How keenly the white Assembly vote
in bills, nooses around black throats
protecting order – zeal equal
only to their distaste for all
spending on Black health. Did they lament
Black children dying of malnourishment?
Tax food imports, make cuts in wages;
ignore the deaths, Black mothers' rages.
More law and order! Who can forget
the raging outbreaks: measles, small pox,

dysentery, yellow fever, whooping cough?
How it took the unbiased sword
of cholera to force an Act? Not a word
till after 20,000 breathed
their last; only then did they concede
expenditure on public health
might in the end protect their wealth.
Now, five days of continuous labour
equals a year's hire. This to ensure,
intimidating boots resound
as the police comb Black compounds.
Contracts change from one year to a month,
but bring to Blacks no real growth.
Wages reduced for each day absent.
Housing levies a hefty rent.

2.

Shingled, painted chattels built
from used wood, to be moved at will,
if ordered by massa off his land
when he no longer needs the hired hand,
or by workers seeking better wages,
these shacks have, though lasting ages,
a transient look, always on the run.
Perched on stone piles, with one
room only, doors front and back,
humble, but treated with no lack
of pride, broomed clean, inside and out
like others lining the dirt road.
Sun-bleached clothes, laid out like hope,
mottle the nut grass. A wash tub
cradles a scrubbing board that sits
atop a bucket. As he thinks befits
some style, a young man in a felt hat
leans eased against the house to chat
with passers-by. Languid, stern, no

neighbour disrespects him as they go.
These tenantries allow small plots
for growing provisions, neat spots
of green around these Black folk's homes.
But though there's access to Barbados loam
no Black can purchase freehold land,
except some planter frees his hand.
(Circled perhaps by death, grateful
for their protection, the occasional
planter bequests ex-slaves a fair
portion of his wealth.) Such acts, rare
as justice, take years to reach Black hands.
Yet, one who's hooked to the island's
future, remembering forebears'
endurance through the centuries,
stoic, will wait for twenty years.
Each cheque paid for a lot on old
Rock Hall creates the first freehold
village. In Workman's, scene's similar;
land at last to the patient tiller
whose love for freedom's evident
in the cartful's of produce sent
to market. But on the estate,
the planter still controls the ex-slaves' fate.

3.
In shadeless fields, bent scarred men hack
then head the cane – tied to the rack
of the broiling sun – load up mule
and ox carts, feeding endless fuel
to mills and vats for boiling juice.
Whipped by the driver's crude abuse,
there's grumbling by the much aggrieved
or the hurt silence of the long deceived.

Outside their chattels, hucksters load
provisions for the weary road
to town: in tunic of sugar bags
an old man, pad of rags
on his head, awaits his burden.
He hails a sharp-faced woman,
head-tied, holding a whip. She's driver
of the estate's child gang. Daughter
or wife? It's hard to say;
harsh labour drains all youth away.

4
In the city, Nancy Daniels,
African-born domestic dwells,
head-tied, wrapped in dress and shawl
of silk brocade, makes her daily call
on God, her thick-veined hands clutching
her leather-bound Bible, lifting
her eyes veiled with cataract's stain
or from seeing too much pain.
Hubert, the fiddler, in rolled-up,
holely, hand-me-downs lash-up
from the White family who feeds him,
shakes an old rheumatic limb
for a salesman leaving a Broad
Street haberdasher's, plucks a chord
for a woman when her brougham stops.
For just twelve cents a tune, he strops
his strings, smiles his 'much-obliged' smile,
entertainer in the old-days style.
When the sun is highest in the sky
he finds an overhanging balcony
on Swan Street where, dozing in the shade,
he dreams another life where wealth is made
from his one tune and many songs.
Nearby, a huckster, old but strong,

70

reaches the city, balancing her load
of yams on her padded head-tied head.
She finds her usual place to stay
bends creaking, putting down her tray,
lays a crocus bag on the ground,
piles her yams in a tempting mound,
cuts one in half: bonus to retain
some faithful buyer. If it rains,
she'll wear the brown bag as a hood,
cover the produce best she could.
Down at the Wharf, barefooted men
weigh sugar on the steelyard scales, then
stack the sealed barrels for export.
Young boys with skillets, making sport,
catch over-spills, a laughing band,
lick-off the sweetness on their hands.

CHAPTER EIGHT

1.
But there was one who would not rest
while Black Barbadians were oppressed.
With a patrician forehead and nose,
deep-set steady eyes, mouth firm closed,
pursed with concern, curved at the side,
a gentleness that served to hide
a certainty that had no doubt,
a fearlessness in speaking out
for Blacks against the white doctrine
(despite his own smooth 'passing' skin,
the outcome of a planter's rape –
a power no woman could escape)
of white man's power without end.
Here was one who would not bend,
Samuel Jackman Prescod,
who gladly took up Bussa's rod
and struck it on the harsh slave yard.
He knew Black voices shouting, 'Lawd!'
(despised by whites as a lesser breed),
expressed true essence of the Christian creed.
He told the aches of freed Black toil,
his *Liberal* leaves found fertile soil
in shaping hopes, through legal means,
for Blacks to have some part in dreams
for the future shaping of our rock:
a citizenry of all Bajan stock.
He taught true freedom always comes
from the receipt of power, not rums.
Put property, franchise, lands
into the care of labouring hands,
or else they'll strike, he warns Glenelg,
until their civil rights are upheld,
so they can travel where they choose.

He knew MacGregor's bitter use
of 'poison' to define Black struggle
was ironically quite true
from a white man's jaundiced point of view.
And though he didn't see our full franchise,
for white clouds still controlled the sky's
blue expanse (alias the BDA),
Prescod knew they could not always stay
the tide for a Crown Colony,
plans supported by Lord Hennessy,
would one year find Blacks nearer the sun
and massa lamenting that his day was done.

2.

Mid-April arches like a cat
alarmed and ready for combat,
whiskers a-quiver. On the tense streets
clenched stones and tramping feet
stride towards drawn, glinting weapons.
The sun's fury rides and hardens
over massa's house and fields of cane.
The skyline floods with choking skeins
of smoke. Below, those clenching stones,
like prowling enraged lions,
seize food through smashed-down wooden doors
from terrified brown merchants in their stores.
Between high and low, a rare rapport
as workers riot in support
of Governor Pope-Hennessy
and the Leeward isles confederacy,
for the chance for work on other isles.
But such alliances are not the style
of governors, and dismissing
liberal sentiment, the juggling
Pope-Hennessy pulls back, regroups
the ruling class, sends in the troops.

Five days later, the police claim
peace restored. London wonders who to blame
for this outburst of the masses,
conclude their man was one of those jackasses,
arrogant and cock-up prone,
but still the chap's one of their own;
such jobs are meant to be life long
so off they pack him to Hong Kong.

3.
But long years passed and little changed
the social order was not rearranged.
The caveat Act would go unheeded.
The caveat Report would go unread.
The caveat Commission was ignored.
The caveat hurricane struck while planters snored.
Wearing such blinkers who would glimpse
the ex-slaves moving to apocalypse?
Death rode in on its steed of misery:
small pox, fever, dysentery
engraved the bodies of the working class,
a portrait on a hidden canvas,
mocked by sky's backdrop of blue,
blue sea – blue grinding labour too.
Into that dry-bones season comes
news of a king's approach. Mandingo drums
announce his royal advance
to Bajan soil. Here was the chance
to see a true black shining king.
For some it was enough to bring
the grand thought that, if not
in their time, in their children's, the blot
of servile pasts would be erased,
and a new lineage would be raised
to soaring heights, like a hawk set free.

King Jaja landed. A day of jubilee.
In a blue suit like a clean but worn
sea admiral's uniform,
he rose from the deck of the *Pylades*
a sailor weathered by the seas.
At the wharf, after a searching glance
he arced his hand in a regal stance,
light leaping from his brow. A fount-
ain of applause rose from the waterfront.
Four old men, vigour roused with zeal,
pound out praise on instruments of steel,
penny-whistle, snaredrums, bass.
Excitement on each glistening face,
as sweat rolls down with force of war
they knock against white rule's closed door,
hammering hard to pry open a space
for this king, moving with limping grace
on to the teeming waterfront,
whose presence made their spirits mount.
Though they'd expected him to be
in African robes, they gladly
cheered his footfall on the Wharf's south side,
one of their own, a source of pride.
The borders of his hair were shaved
into a wide rolling 'M' that made
his forehead seem larger than it was.
The clean-shaved face had painful hollows
at the cheeks, though his regal bearing
and steady, deep-set eyes scouring
this foreign place, made all aware
how much dignity a man could bear.
Passing clustered barrels of rum
and sugar, the Navy guards come
to lead him through the gathered horde,
all thirsty to hear just one word
from the king. Jaja pointed to a dark

tall man and said: 'Good people, mark
my words. The son of that man's son
one day will lead this people on
to glory.' The crowd buzzed with awe
at this king's certainty and power.
Whispering, they looked around
to see to whom the gracious sound
of Jaja's voice was directed.
'He mean Mr. Barrow,' a woman pointed,
'holding he little boy Reginald.
Praise be, wunna future's told!'
An old woman, once a house slave
at Bayley's, swore with a hand-wave
to heaven that this King Jaja
was the spitting image of Bussa.
Only coming from that ancient line
could make again a man so fine.
Limping but graceful, Jaja reached
his waiting carriage, waved to each
and every member of the crowd.
The responding cheers were loud
that followed the clippety-clop
of the speeding vehicle. To the top
of Bay Street the people pursued;
Jaja, felt touched, his kingship renewed.
But in his carriage, even at rest,
he winces as pains lance his chest
each time he coughs, sweat glistening
on his drawn face. The listening
guards wish uneasily for the journey's end.
Through the carriage window, the salt wind
cools. Jaja counts twenty-six fortresses
along that coast. The sentences
he received, expulsion and exile,
pain him more than the bronchial
disease that grips him firm.

The carriage slows, takes a left turn
through a machineel-lined road,
stops by the stone steps of the fort.
Would he be quartered here with British troops?
The thought made him scowl and cheupse.
Patience, companion in St. Vincent,
threatened suicide rather than be sent
by sea with him or to Opobo.
A new love? He felt that fear grow
like a boil. The carriage turns north
on roads lined with flame trees and rows
of exclaiming palms, past the house
of the Governor who'd arranged this route.
They crawl a hill for over a mile
that winds like his thoughts of exile –
that rupture from the balm of home.
The carriage stops. He sees a name
on a house – 'Walmer Cottage'.
Here, there are stables, a carriage
and cow house, a trinity of bedrooms,
baths, servants quarters. But the room
where they put his things feels like a tomb
(though it is comfortable, clean),
haunted by something cold, unseen.
At the doors, surly guards take turns
to tramp night and day. Potted ferns
in the hallway echo his thoughts,
their serrated edges and the warts
of spores suggest the cuts that test,
the spreading sickness in his chest.
Alone, he misses his many wives,
but what hurts most are the drifting lives
of his leaderless people. Fast
his spirit ebbs, a sign the die is cast;
it soon will fly from sore rib cage
over the sea to his ancestral village.
In his mind, he sees the surging

waves beat on Needham's beach, his longings
to escape this Bajan prison
caught by a sail feathering the horizon.

Next day, to try to cut his gloom,
his jailers send a woman to his room
to attend his needs, a local girl
named Becka, her hair done up in curls.
Daily, she massages him, sings island
songs whose traces of African
rhythm gladdens his ailing heart.
He grows to like her. Once, she sits too far
down his thigh and his swollen knees
howl in pain. For days, no ease.
From then on she only sits next to him.
She grows used to hearing his refrain –
'You will go with me to Opobo' –
but still young Becka didn't know
what to say. She looks at his serious
face and, not to make him feel worse,
Becka gets up and she's laughing,
her colourful pinafore whirling
around the room. 'Jaja, I got
dis song fo' you, ready or not.'

'King Jaja won' leh Becka 'lone,
King Jaja won' leh Becka 'lone,
King Jaja won' leh Becka 'lone,
Wha' Becka got, um is all she own.

If yuh want to live in sin,
Get a lil' house an' put me in.
And if yuh start to play de fool,
Ah'll get a big stick an' keep yuh cool.

King Jaja won' leh Becka 'lone,
King Jaja won' leh Becka 'lone,

King Jaja won' leh Becka 'lone,
Wha' Becka got, um is all she own.

If yuh love me treat me nice,
An' I will cook you peas and rice,
But if yuh start to play de fool,
Ah'll get a big stick an' keep yuh cool.

King Jaja won' leh Becka 'lone,
King Jaja won' leh Becka 'lone,
King Jaja won' leh Becka 'lone,
Wha' Becka got, um is all she own.'

Jaja laughs. Although his body ached,
he feels his spirit being touched.
But the joys of laughter also provoke
his thoughts of home, his lost kinfolk,
and much to Becka's sad surprise,
she sees tears falling from his eyes.
She puts her hand on his shoulder.
Jaja looks to her so much older.
'Wha' wrong, Jaja. I did only mekking sport.'
His dreaming eyes are pooled with hurt.
She sits beside him on the couch,
ready to listen to the old man's grouch.

'We made it clear from well before
they start, they must obey our law.
For three centuries they complied.
Tenure ended, they either left or died.
Then they seized the palm oil trade
and chiefs sucked up to them, made
greedy deals that put in hock our land,
sent their sons to school in England,
who returned to us like white ghosts
who'd lost all that mattered most.
Their consuls, turning into thiefs,
poked into our affairs, sided with chiefs

who'd let them have their way,
exploited any tendency to betray.
This imposture had to be rolled
back, or my face was in a bowl
of cow's dung. So I start to resist
from hinterland to coast.
Then comes the bad-talk – and my troubles start
to chafe against my weary heart.
They called me tyrant, upstart savage,
who should be humbled, banished.
When French and Germans make footfall
in our land, with greedy jackal
underlook, now comes the offer
from our British 'friends' to secure
us by having a Protectorate,
supposedly designed to gate
our rights from those foreign traders.
I didn't trust those devious spiders
and carefully questioned each clause.
Assured 'protection' did not cause
loss of sovereignty, I signed.
I could not know that mine
and ten other chiefly signatures
would lead us to the forfeiture
of our land. This, they said, was now
part of the British Empire. How
diabolical! I vowed to fight
it how I could. Then one night
the gunboats came. Johnson called me
to a meeting. For a long day
that devil I resist. Then the threat
that trapped me in the British net
to raze my land with warships. I
gave in and wrote Salisbury
these lines: 'We know the Germans
in the Cameroons took such action,

but never thought for a moment
this could be done by your Government.'
I had faith in the higher authority
in London. Was this just naivete?
I felt there was a just ruler
who respected the rights of others.
Johnson now slyly sought allies
against me by spreading invidious lies,
then set devious plans to catch
me at a meeting he then hatched.
He promised me that I'd be free
to go once I'd heard his parley.
Why did I trust the white man's oath?
Next morning, as the sun rose
over Opobo, a score of war
canoes, throbbing with drums for our
journey set out. Women and children
danced and sang to speed our mission.
The flotilla advanced towards
the bank to the waiting British guards.
I neared the shore. My war canoe,
The Queen, advanced alone, moving through
the guards. Then I saw British guns
swing towards Opobo town.
I was told to surrender or face
destruction of my natal place.
Johnson gave me an hour to decide.
Defeat unthinkable, our heads held high,
my chiefs favoured confrontation.
I thought of my favourite son
in England, my town across the river.
So I went with the consul, giver
of false oaths, to the *Goshawk*; then
to Bonny I was taken,
where they put me on the *Calabar*,
a mail steamer sailing for Accra.

From there, I sent off telegrams
to friends in England. Now the sham
was clear, for they imprisoned me
and convened the rude mockery
of a trial. My spirits fell.
English contacts proved an empty shell;
my only comfort that I was
yet on African soil – because,
though difficult, I could still send
messages to my chiefs and friends,
know of affairs in Opobo.
But comfort was brief, and then, oh
my grief was coffin-deep. When
would I see my family again?
For Johnson I felt only hatred,
a man's word in our world is sacred,
as good as his life.
                              In a mirror
in my room I saw a creature
in a European suit who
wasn't me, saw a face of pallid hue,
ashen like a man who is dead.
Patience and my boy Sunday paid
a visit next day. For a long while
I hugged my boy. My fate was exile
to a place called the West Indies
far over cold isolating seas.
I begged that Sunday be sent
to cold England as a student.'
He paused. Becka saw his dry lips,
fetched him water. He took two sips,
asked if she wanted to hear more.
She said, 'Jaja, man, are you sure
you don't want to rest awhile?'
He'd go on. She gave a rueful smile.
'I ended up on St. Vincent,

82

kept in touch with home through letters sent
to my son, instructing him to
write his mother, get all the news,
and, in particular, let me know
what was happening in Opobo.
One joy: Sunday made it through the seas
to England to complete his studies.
I wrote the Queen, pleading with tears
for return home to spend my last years
fanned by the wind of my native land.
The Queen, alas, did not respond,
choosing to overlook my aid
in the Ashanti Wars – the Sword
of Honour she gave still in my house.
St. Vincent turned sour in my mouth:
dinner parties, soirees at Government House.
Most of those longing days I spent
watching the sea's endless lament,
gazing at the empty horizon.
Never had I felt so alone.
I contracted pneumonia
and this crippling melancholia,
even begged the chemist for poison.
Now doctors urged I be sent home,
and though Whitehall quietly agreed,
the British holding me would not concede.
As my health grew daily worse,
my fear was exile's dreadful curse,
for how can ancestors receive a soul
unless buried in native soil?
I hatched a plan to escape by boat;
it was betrayed, never got afloat.
Like sharp cane blades the month's grew long;
I neither ate nor slept; all along
I sensed the British want me dead,
but not to have the guilt upon their head.

The next thing I get to hear was
I was being transferred to Barbados.'
Jaja stopped. Becka's honest tears
came in jerking sobs. She drew near,
hugged him, got him ready for bed.
Then she sat and stroked his head,
humming a slow island melody,
grieved to see such lone infirmity.
When she heard the old man snore
She softly left and closed the door.

The sun rose over the island
and Jaja rose with it, still warmed
by the relief telling his story
had brought. Around nine-thirty,
in his sea admiral's outfit,
he prepared for a courtesy visit
to Parliament. Knowing the press
would come, he'd seize the chance to address
the people, speak of his misfortune,
let his kidnapping be publicly known.
The steel-tired carriage rattled down
Bay Street, then across the Chamberlin
Bridge, past Careenage's bobbing masts,
the Public Buildings reached at last,
where he's impressed to see the tower
with its chiming clock to sound the hour;
then they cross Trafalgar Square,
into the buildings' courtyard where,
sweating in the rising morning's heat,
Bajans have assembled to greet
the king they're curious to see.
Jaja limped to the outer balcony
with his cane, raised a hand to quell the roar.
When he spoke his voice was sure.
'I, a king of a sovereign country

stripped of my kingship, no longer free,
an exile, political prisoner;
now from one island to another,
I'm like unwanted baggage sent.
Why do I merit such treatment?
To be deprived of my country,
my markets, my freedom, is contrary
to the spirit of the British nation
which ordered slavery's abolition.'
The guards, overtaken by surprise,
only now move to hush his cries,
gently steer him from the crowd's hot breath
as though concerned only for his health.
At the back of the packed courtyard,
Becka shouted and clapped him hard.
To have heard this she feels blessed,
as pride grows swelling in her breast.

Next day, Jaja awoke before sunrise,
tried to get up, found he couldn't rise,
his muscles throbbing with rheumatic ache,
life ebbing with each bronchial intake
of breath. Fearing he's about to die,
he's rushed to be examined by
three doctors. Their alarming report
confirmed that Jaja's kidneys, heart
and lungs were all diseased.
With new despondency he's seized.
He craved death to let his spirit go,
not here, not here, but in Opobo.

4.
Meantime, Governor Sendall,
between sips of tea, reads out all
Jaja's address to his lady wife.
His yearning's for a quiet life,

and, steeped in the marital formality
of their time, they share the ceremony
of the afternoon's Earl Gray.
Standing outside the half-closed door
(who knows when they might ask for more?)
a female servant hears Sendall say,
'It's not good to prolong his stay.
Our negroes do not need to hear
what Jaja said. It could lead, I fear,
to trouble. One must pluck that weed.'
'We can't have that,' his wife agreed.
'That would be a catastrophe...
Walter, what might they *do* to me?'
Mrs. Sendall gave her husband
a long accusing stare, one hand
rivered with bluish veins, clasping
the other, her bottom lip wobbling.
'Jaja's life has almost run its course,
if he dies here our credit will be worse.'
Sendall's voice sounded almost sad,
for, secretly, he'd been impressed
by Jaja's charm and kingly look.
Later, in his study, he took
out paper, drafted a telegram
expressing his reason for concern.
He was sure, he told the FO,
Jaja should now be shipped to Opobo.
FO agreed, but needed a few months
to establish British dominance.
Sendall summoned Jaja, gave him tea,
said, 'We'll soon have you put to sea,
but you must give your solemn pledge,
signed and sealed on this page,
not to resist us in Opobo.'
Jaja wanted to tell him 'No!'
but feels entrapped, seeing the face

of the solemn, stolid Queen laced
with indifference, her portrait's
lifeless eyes that coldly calculate
an empty life since Albert's passing,
immune now to Jaja's suffering,
his dying need for home.
His jaw tight, Jaja left the room.

The night before he had to sign
his surrender, Jaja dreamed
he was in a room coiled like a foetus
on a bed. A bull terrier barks
at the figure of a man who lurks
hovering over him. From the shape
of the forehead, there's no mistake
the visitor is his father,
who leaves, beckons him to follow after.
'You British want to kill me,' Jaja tells
Sendall next day. 'Last night, I close
my eyes. Saw my father and my dog.
The next one I see will be God.'

5.
Free at last to return, Jaja
never made it back to Africa,
reaching only the Canary isles
the final soil of his exile.
When they heard of his death on Tenerife,
Black Bajans shared Opobo's grief.
All the island's minstrels sang
of Jaja and Becka. Songs rang
through every dusty village street.
Tuk Bands played, people stomped their feet.

CHAPTER NINE

1.
City to country, brick to soil.
Commerce to cane field, counting to toil.
Flesh to flesh and bone to bone.
Blood to blood and blood alone.
A story as old as commerce,
merchant money buys bucolic earth:
Planters tried to save their lands
by selling assets to local merchants,
so estates going under with debt
need not be sold on the London market –
their own Chancery would keep them afloat.
Through outright purchases and bad debts,
through strategic marriages for land
that came with a planter's daughter's hand,
merchants bought estates and bought respect
that edged them closer to state power,
long controlled by old-time planter.
So a mercantile beast had grown
fat with political acumen.
Now he sits with godhead pompous
(fondling his planter bride a bonus)
on statutory boards, legislative
councils, on vestries, executive
boards and various committees,
on the floors of assemblies....
Coloured merchants held token benches,
men like Lofty and the Lynches.

For Blacks, the same old Bajan tune,
so much life extinguished all too soon,
hustled to unmarked rab-land graves,
the final resting place for slaves.
Though when times could not get harder,

a kind of rescue came from Panama
when the Canal's door swung open with demand
for labour. Bajans heard the sound,
seized the doorknob, entered, found
the eager steamers linking Bridgetown
and Colon. From each buzzing platform,
sweating profusely under the sun,
Blacks cursed Whites as they went out.
On every trip you'd hear them shout:
We want good wages, we want dum now.
We want good wages, and we know how
to get dum. Yankees pay man like a man.
Yuh won't gi' we good wages so we to Pan-
ama. Planters found a way around, of course:
replacing men with women's labour force;
centralizing sugar refining when
they brought in the efficient vacuum-pan,
and steam to drive the rollers round
for some time kept their profit-levels sound.
Then came the longest years
of fall and the Bajan planters' tears
as they heard the scuttling feet
of Europe's merchants buying beet.
To keep their lifestyles in the same old way,
they slashed slave wages below slave wage,
(though when the Great War flattened beet,
Massa stumbled back to his feet).

But Blacks could not forget the African king
and how the sea and sky both seemed to ring
as he stepped onto the waterfront,
not those three boys scarce able to count
who were touched by Jaja's shadow
as he moved through the crowd –
Rawle, Clennell, and Charles – still in the grip
of his majesty. Now, at the docking of the Ship,

where cabins were filled with the working class,
and fathers were Blues and mothers Stars,
their future as leaders of the masses
was taking shape. They forecast Garvey's ways,
his organizing skills, knew they were Africans,
could relate to the struggling man
and woman the discipline of a saving's plan.
Stars in white, starch-stiff uniforms
men in naval blue. The ship steers
towards its members' needs. They had no fear
of sickness or death, for weekly deposits,
legally drawn, covered such benefits.
Members were buried in military style:
marching bands in grand processions. Meanwhile
some churches changed to meet black people's
needs, gave chances for self-leadership,
discipline, morality, respect,
though white-washed clergy got real vexed,
denounced the masses' search
for relevance as bringing devils into Church.
Still, the Ship rolled on, draped in faith;
a labour union, and a
democratic league, a working
men's association – all growing.
The warrior musicians, the Tuk band,
the Land Ship's well-tuned engine.

CHAPTER TEN

1.

Rawle, Clennell and Charles comprised
my first self. I, Grantley, the second.
I barely remembered educator Rawle,
and I was cause of Clennell's fall
when I destroyed him in a planter's
libel suit. His *Herald* staggered
in disgrace, slaughtered by my Oxford
acumen and planters' support.
Charles bore the weight of workers' hopes –
and my unceasing, sniping blows,
until worn down he died of fatigue,
and with him went the Democratic League.
I knew there were other selves:
two, yet nameless, lurked in the shadows,
selves to be controlled like the wild
worker hot-heads full of envious bile.
Though I thought as the planters thought,
such Blacks eyed me, as if I could be bought
by their wheedling looks. One had the gall
to say, 'You'll come around. After all,
you're one of us. When you taste racism's
bitter root, you'll turn towards us.
Our people need a brain like yours.'
Those words kept ringing through the hours
as I sensed my other selves swallow them,
dark forms that kept those ominous
words alive in me, growing in the shadows.
All this one morning after an
Assembly meeting, the sun vaporous
with April's threat of rain. Four of us
talked in the courtyard. A stocky rep
from the working class (whose name I forget)
strolled to my ear with his prophecy,

at once a threat and a humble plea.
My two grandfathers locked their fists,
one white, one black. Ancestral mists
coiled in sinuous fighter's grace
inside my head. I had to turn my face,
gradually, and against my trembling will,
towards my Black grandfather until
I heard my voice demand education
for all children, abolition
of child labour, and, to my surprise,
the workers' rights to unionize.
Speaking now for those who of old
I'd helped oppress, I accepted their cold
response and the surprised, uncertain eye
of those who tightly gripped the economy.
But when workers grow restless as waves
it is himself a wise man saves,
for bobbing on that raging sea can harm:
I swam again for safety to white arms.

2.
Features grew on my third self's shadow,
this self that was a puzzle to me. Now,
confidently, he raised both hands
and, shedding conception's cautious bands,
he burst into the world aflame.
I'd watch this Clement make his name;
from the back of every crowd,
I watched him with a sibling scowl.
To most, it seemed, that Clement
had sprung from nowhere, caffuffling them
with the mystery of his birth.
To them, he'd suddenly appeared on earth,
a grown man. But I knew he'd come
from Trinidad – to Bajan parents born.
Schooled here from the age of four,

worked as a clerk in his late-teen years,
'til his return to Trinidad where,
moved by the workers' tears,
he joined Garvey's U.N.I.A.
and, later, the N.W.C.S.A
under whose political influence
he returned to us. Some marked his strange
accent: 'Where you come from?' 'Who name
you?' 'You sound like a Trini.' 'We doan care.
Talk yuh talk. We list'ning.' 'You're
de unly politician who know how we feel.'
'That Grantley like he want all we to kneel
before massa like in de ole-time days.
He got too much o' de white man ways.'
'We want we rights; we want dum now.
If we doan get dum, we gine show
them some sport.' 'Yes, we want we rights;
we want dum now.' I sighed
when that worker cursed my name.
Sweat broke out on me. For the first time shame,
though I'd long known they didn't trust
me. Could I blame them? I had thrust
myself into white arms, destroyed Black
leaders, married an English lass.
The fact was, Clement and I were one.
This thought unbalanced me, drove me insane.
Crouched in disguise, at meetings under
city streetlights circled by moths, in wonder,
I saw his following grow, saw
them drawn like fireflies, ready to make war
if he willed it. The curled waves of his hair
brushed back, the youthful, visionary stare,
his fiery tongue lifting their hopes
beyond the encircling ropes
of poverty. Poor wages, price inflation,
weak trade unions, victimization,

the wickedness of race discrimination,
the Italian invasion of Ethiopia
and the white Barbadian's negrophobia.
All, he convinced his listeners, could be altered.
I hoped he knew he was in danger.
Yet, if he knew, I sensed it was too late;
his mission was locked to him by fate.
His voice echoed through Golden Square
and the Lower Green; out from bare
hovels the hungry thousands came.
It wasn't long before his name
reached Government, who soon stopped
his meetings; watched him round-the-clock.
Like ol' haigs they eyed him, but he wouldn't relent.
One morning, five officers were sent
to bring him before the City Magistrate.
The date for a rush trial was set,
accusing him of making false
claims that Barbados was his birth place,
I refused his plea, sent him to defend himself.
He couldn't pay so why expose myself?
He lost, filed an appeal, headed for Golden
Square where he denounced his conviction
to a crowd of thousands. He was their great
messiah crucified. Next day,
a Friday throbbing with heat, Clement
and 300 marched to Government
House singing hymns and anthems.
Before the House, my other self
alone advanced towards the gate
sentried by armed police. 'For your life's sake,
don't make another step,' the Deputy
Inspector General said, brusquely
grim, winked to a heavy-jawed lawman
who advanced with cuffs in his hand.
Thirteen rushed to Clement's rescue

and were arrested, too. I had to do
something. Clement was of my blood.
Inspired, I'd now do anything I could.
'You'll come around,' the worker's rep had said.
'You're one of us.' So I defended
him in Appeal and won.
Let the Royal Commission
know the rebellion's cause: lack
of decent living conditions for Black
people. Now, Clement's triumph brought
out thousands jubilant to the Court,
there to escort him home. Too late.
They'd secretly slipped him through a gate,
(action you'd think the verdict would disbar),
then detectives stuffed him in a car,
and whisked him away. Crowds lined
Pier Head waterfront hoping to find
and even rescue their leader.
Deception's breath poisoned the air.
Clement wasn't placed on the vessel
at Pier Head; police had hustled
him out through Carlisle Bay. This known,
the masses struck at Golden Square with stones,
sharp broken bottles, and hard sticks.
Flames leapt exclaiming from smashed car windows.
Street lamps popped, fizzled and groaned,
circuits broken by the fury of stones.
From a broken hydrant water spewed
onto a fast-flooding alley stewed
with rage. Black police in riot array
arrived. The night was a funny day.
Like a cinder roused by the wind,
in the morning riots flared again.
Old-time weapons smashed through
office fronts and store windows. Few
cars remained upright. Black hands seized

pale gasping Mutual employees,
briefly held them hostage,
threatened to burn them in their offices.
Along Bay Street and Probyn Street,
the masses' carnival moved to one beat,
then crossed Chamberlain Bridge where
two pariahs glance furtively, aware
of some impending doom, then scurry
behind safe crates lining the Wharf. Giddy
with rage, rebels charged through the Square
onto Broad Street. And it was there
a collective sigh sliced through
the ages, joined ancestors to new
warriorhood. But just as glimpsed
the ancestral vision faded
when armed police with bayonets
advance, and from the shadows marksmen pick
off marchers. With no answer to state guns
Blacks fell and died. Others ran
for their lives through city alleys
where rats patrolled in twos and threes.

Black rage spread to the countryside,
looting potato fields and any food they spied,
threatening staff. Armed police follow
the retaliative scent, with force restore
a tense calm as when dry leaves settle
after a furious gust. The fatal
truth is they're more scattered, hurt,
embittered and ready to subvert.
Fourteen died, three hundred tried,
convicted, and often beaten. No Whites died.
Better for Clement to be deported
than to be dead, I thought, divided
to the vein. I'd felt my feelings lurch
like some prodigal to the workers' hearth,

but what future could there be for me
connected to the masses' anarchy?
Planters now saw me as a voice for Blacks.
I would need protection from attacks,
So I met with Governor Young
(who had signed Clement's expulsion
in spite of the dropped charges), shook his hand.
Afterwards, I packed and left for England
where Ormsby-Gore took a liking to me,
and began to allay the planters' incredulity.
I returned home with the blessings
of the C.O.. My cunning wings
spread and flapped. I was leader now
of the labour movement, but somehow
also regained white planter trust –
I stamped all militants into dust.
Clement was gone, exiled to Trinidad.
I admit his deportation made me glad.
I was now an island, its width and depth.
But there in the shadows lurked my fourth self,
still featureless, unable yet to say its name,
yet burning each day with a hotter flame.

CHAPTER ELEVEN

1.
A new moon rose over the island.
Sea breezes from the south rolled inland
through the trellised balcony of my home
on Spooner's Hill, over the cobbled limestone
yard, through gardens of lantana,
bougainvillea, allamanda.
Spider lilies danced around
the whitewashed base of a royal palm,
with votive crotons, an hibiscus hedge.
Red ixoras raged in flaming beds,
burnt rows of 'Match-Me-Nots', brown and green,
each leaf a different tone and sheen.
Bougainvillea took a carmine sprawl
behind the encircling iron wall.
Flamboyants sentried my home
at three points, each red uniform
circled by its fleeing lover's scent,
sweet and bloody, love's relinquishment.
Swells of variegated immortelles
reminded me of my duelling selves,
a battle still not quite over.
Yet, I sensed race pride could cover
a multitude of crimes to self:
hypocrisy, treachery, worship of wealth.

Over the sea-green lawn raced my joy,
fifth self, a scrawny fair-skinned boy,
protected now but groomed for politics.
So he would know the world I let him mix
with poor but decent neighbourhood boys
and learn the art of making up free toys.
They'd career about the grounds, play
cockfight with quartered mahogany

pods, each sharp-beaked tip a hook
one's competitor tried to break.
Once, I saw him zigzagging between
the variegated immortelles to spin
an imaginary web, until, breathless,
he fell on the flamboyant's fallen dress
entranced by all that giddying blood,
its iridescent monthly flood.
I was beginning to know happiness
against this backdrop of familial bliss.
I joined with others to diminish
merchant-planter power. Progress
we all desired, but on the how we split;
league in name but no real unit.
Seale objected to my crablike pace,
called me a traitor to my race,
my colonial moderation was too slow,
too much a compromise. We had to grow
deeper bases before demanding swift reform,
I felt. Moving too fast could only harm
the cause. So, wild horses like Seale
had to be reined in, brought to heel.
The challenge to my tactical reserve
came when Garveyite Seale had the nerve
to summon a strike with all his lavish
rhetoric of Black consciousness.
The tightrope quivered beneath my foot.
My arms clawed the air to find some hold.
I saw great things on the horizon.
How could I let his rashness pitch me down?
How let them slate me in the planter press
for all Seale's idiocy — ask more, get less?
In secret, my self-saving instinct sent
me to secure support from government;
then win support of moderate colleagues
and force Seale's resignation from the League.

When the executive proposed to give
him money for his services,
I denounced their complicity with his
hot-headedness. Although not by design,
my vehemence forced them to resign.
Around me now were purring loyalists
who fanned me with one endless yes.
The tightrope stretched ahead to victory
One arm to lift the people, the other, me.

2.

In January came Lord Moyne,
earnest, ready for change. My ploy,
to put the case for nationalizing
sugar factories, didn't make him wince.
(My aim: to find out what the C.O.
was ready to concede. But go
that way? That was not my line:
gradual concessions over time
was saner. That way I had the space
to build a structure, a future base.
I was President of the League
and the Union's first President,
my voice unchallenged in both houses.
And though some other hotheads set
a Congress up to challenge us,
no-one could politic like me:
make worker, planter or government
official feel I shared, could represent
their point of view. I soothed their cries,
so on the day we got full franchise
and Cabinet rule we were best placed to rise
to win the people's vote and take the prize.
The League (now renamed the BLP) won
control of Government in fifty-one.
But there was to be no peace in heaven;

rebels and renegades arose in
dubious battle in both my houses.

First to emerge was my fourth self,
now fully formed, risen from the dark,
a radical scowl lighting his path.
They didn't know Barbados like me.
Such swiftness, such extremity,
would only abort the calm dream
of peaceful reform. What may seem,
or is just will only consummate
with the right time. Those who can't wait
are victims of the politics of lust.
Those who love the world wait for *le temp juste*.
My patience flapped into cerulean sky
and vanished. Then I swooped from high
and plucked each disloyal rebel out.
Walcott, my longtime closest aide,
had turned on me his pout
of wounded discontent, said I should
have given him a government post.
Errol, my fourth self, left me to go
his own way. How could I not know
this self would be the one to finish me?
I listened with easy complacency
to his talk of equality and justice,
all that noisy, endless rhetoric.
All talk. I *still* controlled the House.
Now our GOM, how could I refuse
the challenge of the wider Federal stage
through which one country could be made?
Named Federation's first PM,
I left, with springy steps, for Trinidad, then
the capital. I knew my heel was bare,
but I had to go to to take my share
of making the case for integration.

So the Bajan campaign in sixty-one
saw me absent. You know the rest:
Williams and Bustamante end the quest
for West Indian unity.
Back at home, my rebel self, too gladly
building on my absence, ingrate upstart,
denied the father and seized the hearts
of the urban poor, won the election
by a landslide. My public life was done.

I felt as abandoned as the railway line
that once from Bridgetown to Belleplaine
daily carried passengers and produce.
Was I really of no further use?
I retreated to my study for days,
to the comfort of books, to Le Carre's
A Small Town in Germany,
my Dickens' collection, Halsbury's
Laws of England, the pleasure of their smell,
the feel of covers lettered in gold;
the reassurance of my old
editions: Churchill's *World Crisis
of 1915,* the balm there is
in *A Treasury of Kahlil Gibran*.
On my worn mahogany divan
I heard an era's last bells
dying sound as I took brief spells
of rest, gazing through the open
sash windows onto my beloved garden.
When my wife, Grace, called me for tea,
I passed the bronze bust of Cipriani
to meet her by the door and see her smile,
touch her hand and feel its warmth reconcile
me to the calm comforts of home,
the only Eden I could call my own.

CHAPTER TWELVE

1.
I, Grantley's fourth self, had stayed
under his shadow too long. Weighed,
Grantley and lackeys were found too slack.
I gazed out from the patio of my Black
Rock home. My past swam before me, graceful
like sprats circling a reef in measured careful
motion. I recalled the four shillings from
my allowance I gave a cub scout
so he could attend Summer camp;
Canada, where I came of age and learned
to fly in the Royal Air Force,
where I met Carolyn training as a nurse
and took her hand; the sharply creased
airman's trousers I gave a mate in need;
learning the delight in each day's creation
from 45 bombing operations
over Europe's battered cities;
then study at the LSE.
Bar finals; those of my peers I rubbed
up wrong because, they said, I was a snob,
arrogant, 'short' with people; my return
to practice Law and court politics.
So many opportunities overseas,
but I thrilled to smell the salt breeze,
taste rice and peas, hear calypso
and tuk, and bathe in sun's fading glow,
and expectation of its rise tomorrow.

Federation's dissolution grieved me, too,
so, with 8 of the Windwards, we regrouped.
The invidious press called us
'The Little Eight', though there was
nothing little about our dream

of unity. We'd build a team
more lasting than bronze; our capital site
Bim, and I the first head of state.
'Dictatorship!' Grantley shouted,
and the 8 collapsed because we couldn't
agree and Britain refused to commit
to an aid package that met our needs.
They wanted to support us one-to-one.
I said that one from eight leaves none.
Frustrated, one by one, the eight withdrew,
so local freedom from colonial rule
became my party's main priority.
(I confess when talk of independence
within a Federation was raised,
I had nightmares and cold sweats for days.
The whole thing agitated my mind.
I supported Federation's arching vine,
but how could we have a breakthrough
in doing what the Almighty couldn't do:
get Caribbean politicians to unite?
There are more Black humbugs than White.)
I'd made it clear all along that I
opposed imperialism in any guise.
Now, I turned to look in the eyes
of our icy northern 'mother'
to see if there was any hint of ardour.
(The only heat was in her fingers,
dropping colonies like hot potatoes.)
All I found was a selfish mother
who'd squeeze out the best juice before
letting us through the colonial door.
The opposition did their duty,
challenging our vision at every
stage. They'd continue to stay
waiting for direction from the U.K,
as if without confidence to make

their own decisions. Our case we take
to the masses, get their support.
They share our view that Britain ought
to repay the debt slave blood had bought.
We'd have a shortage of capital –
why not broach reparations? Full
payment of all unpaid labour
so we could help the restless poor?
But Britain's gaze lay east, towards
the EEC, not exhausted lands
it no longer wanted. Wasn't this good reason
to broach the subject of reparations
when I met the Secretary of State?
We wanted sovereignty, to be mates
of all, satellites of none. We needed loans,
but could give disciplined production.
We wanted education to be free,
to give our people security,
the chance for all to eat a plate of souse,
the chance of living in a decent house.
But greedy owners asked ridiculous
prices for barren, sapless land,
ignored the offer open in our hands.
And, shaming to our saviour Christ,
the Anglicans endorsed this malice.
(That's why I leaned more to Baptists
and Methodists. Who was for justice?)

The New Year turned. I outlined
to Parliament how Barbados had defined
its own affairs since 1651;
how though others had lived on
handouts from the Colonial Office,
we had never followed this
invidious path. We were ready
for Independence, despite Grantley

who, after the riots of '37,
had suggested to the Royal Commission
a return to Crown Colony status
as his solution to our crisis.
Where the pride? Where the self-respect?
Let the British, who'd broken every ethic,
every law, who'd murdered, raped,
suppressed the language and customs
of our ancestors, feel inferior, not us.

As the sun dropped over Deacons
one evening on my way home,
I passed the whitewashed monument
on the windward side of the seafront
road. I stopped the car, stepped out.
My shadow fell on the busy route
from a red-ants' nest which my cautious
foot avoided. A breeze brought coolness
in from the Shallow Draft, lent
added charm to the monument
on whose towering peak a small white
cross was firmly fixed like the alight-
ing of an ornamental bird.
Night's shadow was falling. I lowered
my eyes to read the inscription
telling of the "first taking of possession
of the island by the English
in 1605." November 30th,
1905 was when it had
been erected. If Whites felt glad
to celebrate this date that meant
Blacks' groaning impoverishment,
we'd seize the time, give it new sense,
make it the date of Independence.

2.

As the days neared when I would meet
with the Secretary of State,
I couldn't sleep. Work was better.
I looked over the draft of my paper
one morning until one o'clock,
left the office, went home, took stock,
made a cup of tea, went to bed,
couldn't stop the panic in my head.
Once I dreamt I was in a canoe
which glided through a veil of mist
towards a foreign shore. Water hissed
and slapped in stark staccato beats
against its sides. The mist retreats
and we're ashore. I hear distant cries:
my people fearful we'll capsize.
I see the British Army guards
have turned their guns towards
Bridgetown's crowded streets. 'There'll be no
reparations; you have to go
it on your own,' the Admiral said.
'Take Independence now. You've no shred
of power to make conditions;
concede, or you face our weapons.'
Whose subject was I to suffer
such a threat? I was no yielder
to massa's bullying. So I refused
to buckle to imperious words.
And then the canon roared. I woke
at once; my sheets in cold sweat soak.
Independence could not be lost
by raising reparations now. I tossed
in bed, rose for another cup of tea.
Deep down I knew that once the deal
was made, it would be a thankless
uphill war for fiscal fairness.

I knew they had us in checkmate,
would punish if we dared to confiscate
from massa's sons who kept their fingers
deep inside the island's limestone purse,
that held the proceeds of *our* labour.
So in speaking to the British,
I was statesmanlike, inclusive.
I refrained from using the terms
'Black' and 'White.' I spoke to them
of Barbadians, joined my voice
with those who with rebellious noise
at Mermaid Tavern had resisted
Cromwell's strutting major-generals.
I invoked that battle as a sign
that our intentions were benign,
of where I saw our democratic
roots, our ballast of historic
tradition in the governing
of our own affairs. On looking
up from my notes, I swear I see
officials winking cynically.
Even the Secretary of State seemed
amused as fleetingly he beamed
at me before returning to
his bored expression. I let him know
that Britain never bailed us out,
for years there'd been no need to turn out
their troops to maintain public order.
In short, we now deserved our
sovereignty. Who could expect
a new country to have no defect?
Slavery had left its bitter taste,
but with goodwill we would erase
those past divisions, raise our poor
through building wealth. Who would explore
modern England with an ancient map?

Secretary Lee gave a clap.
'All we now require from you,' I say,
'is to speed our rendezvous with destiny.'
I left the meeting confident
we would soon be independent.
But leaving down the hallway to
the building's exit, suddenly I go
cold, turn frightened, feeling choked,
as if a hand were at my throat.
I tried to turn, frightened, choked.
I excused myself, entered a toilet,
closed the bowl and sat on it.
The voice of reparations spoke
in me down through time. Guilt invokes
the dusty ancestors calling out
for justice. Why my statesman's doubt?
Too late now to make the demand, I thought.
Such battles would have to be fought
later. Independence came first.
When I'd caught my breath, coerced
that inner voice and re-emerged
to the waiting limo, we all heard
the unspoken deal which was this:
Blacks and Whites would coexist,
they with land and fiscal power,
we with politic's visible hour.
We'd have to let them keep their
ancient wealth; we'd rise through academia,
would prove our ability to Whites
who before long would see it right
to let us stake-hold in their firms.
This would occur on natural terms,
not with the passing of state law.
So when party activists implored
me to help the black middle class, and use
legislative power to induce

race-fair employment practices
and fund Black ownership of businesses,
I clung to my ideal. Despite my stance,
the Whites, amidst Independence
preparations, began an exodus
to the white Commonwealth, showed us
their contempt – and took their money.
Yet still at banks it was a task
to find a Black face at the front desk;
We'd have to do the best we could even while
tied to the slow Westminister style.

I wanted pride in all our nation,
not to hear black people told their station
or see my children branded second class,
or gardener or bus-driver pass
as the summit of a black child's
ambition.
           Back at Downing Street,
I resolved to make past and future meet.
Grey London skies this time wouldn't change
my conviction of the need to rearrange
the class-race nexus of our country.
And though Grantley began to bray
'This leftward move is very shocking.
An appalling state of things...'
bawling 'Dictatorship!' like a record
that's stuck, this time he was ignored.
No one listened to his worry,
Now that we had our own country.

3.
Two days before receipt of formal
instruments, the Hilton Hotel
rose to greet the Duke and Duchess
of Kent. In the packed city's press

of crowds swarming the Careenage,
screams of joy reach the floating barge
where the four Supremes are singing
near the waterfront's edge gleaming
with lights. Screams rise for each shimmy
made in their banded cotton minis,
thin-strapped, pleated, touched with sequins,
gold fluorescent high-heels gliding
over the stage. Their coiffured heads
shake in choreographed glee, spread
joy as their arms wave and arch in
mesmerizing patterns. '*Got him
back in my arms again, right by my side.
Got him back in my arms again... so satisfied.'
'My world is empty without you, Baby.*'
Suddenly, a group of star-crazy
young women rush towards the stage,
forgetting in their star-struck rampage
the stark divide of harbour water.
Shouting, 'Diana! Diana!'
they force a group at the crowd's tip
too close for comfort to the harbour's lip
to the dark reflecting water
that was a nation's rippling mirror.

Next day, applause from Church services;
to the sky, youths' raise clenched fists,
rallying cries from school children
that ring through the rain-washed Garrison.
My girl Lesley, bold as always,
eased away from the VIPs,
moving through mud and slanting rain,
on her face a thrilled expression.
Black boots smacked in pools of water
losing shine, as through the throbbing air
the Police Band's staccato chords

bounce buoyantly through the hordes
who circle milling on the grass.
In one collective stir, a mass
of children, eyes bright like fireflies;
adults driven by pride that rises
on their careworn hopeful faces.
That night, the Church, touching all bases,
offers ecumenical prayers,
and just before midnight, the tears
from heaven cease to fall. The moon
breaks its veil of clouds; emptied, worn
out, they slink off stage. Then moonlight
floods the flagpole where, this night,
in history solemnly savoured,
the Union Jack is lowered
and the sun-held broken trident,
sign of our colonial break, strident
in black, guarded by the blue sea
(our life-giver and our destiny),
inches in glory up the pole.
Flapping and dipping it unfurls
its birthing, dancing in moonlight
to voice freedom's longest night.

CHAPTER THIRTEEN

1
That entire week we hardly slept,
yet, like reef-dwelling sprats we stayed
clear-eyed. Black Rock buzzed with family,
guests and visitors. Young Lesley
and friends feted at the Carlton Club
partying till dawn's glimmer rubbed
the sky; Merrymen and Troubadours
played until December's early hours.
I sought some homelier privacy,
space to reflect upon my odyssey.
The first morning at our new home,
which all of us would call 'The Farm',
I rose to meet new age's dawn.
My family were not awake;
the hidden sun had yet to take
its first steps up the sky. Wrapped
up against the chill, I felt
my way to the back of the Farm
where the animals, snug and warm,
slowly began to stir: some goats,
two cows, a family of rabbits,
chickens, a few pigs, a black-
belly sheep, a pair of waddling ducks.
With bucket I went in the cow
pen, and with remembering hand held low,
emptied her udders of blood-warm milk.
When dawn's filaments of shining silk
threaded with light each waking home,
I smell newness in the air's perfume,
convinced the sea lapping the shore
looked more blue than ever before.

Next day, we left for Bridgetown early,

to get to Cheapside market to buy
the freshest vegetables. There, pigeons
circled our feet, flashed their necks' green
inflorescence, heads forever probing
back and forth in dipping, rocking
rhythm. Absorbed in them I sensed
these birds rustling omniscience.
Back in the car, Carolyn said,
'Errol, that man over there wished
you well, and you ignored him.'
'I didn't mean to be rude,' I replied.
She said, 'I know you're preoccupied
with the weight of the island's future,
but without support from each voter
like that man, however well you plan...'
I listened carefully to her lesson.

2.
In those early years all the zest
of new policy, programmes that stressed
education, tourism, local
manufacturing, healthcare for all;
from sugar we diversified,
developed livestock farming, tried
to raise investment in the economy;
built the Cave Hill campus of UWI.
It was a moderate programme;
nothing to give the Whites alarm.
The '70 Black Power Revolt
in Trinidad led us to act
against hot-heads like Carmichael
whom I thought a preacher of racial
hatred. We didn't need that here.
His words on Black pride, I could share,
but his divisive stance on Black and White
was a fuse too dangerous to light;

there was kindling enough about
to convince us to keep him out.
Our action showed the country's Whites
that while *we* ruled *they* would be alright.

Next year, my old self Grantley died.
I could find no tears, would have lied
to say that his demise upset,
gave me one moment of regret.
To me, for twenty years, hostile
abuse had been his public style.
No hypocrite, I could not mourn
or even attend the funeral.
This first misreading of the Bajan
mindset cost me dear. To a man
(and woman) my honesty was viewed
as rank filial ingratitude.
'Heartless', 'callow' were among the sticks.
Silent, I had to take the licks.

3.
Bright morn turned to cloudy day;
storms brewed in the economy.
The World Bank made us tighten belts,
a squeeze that had to be passed on
to the people through high taxation.
At this moment, Grantley's fifth self
jumped onto the political shelf,
out from his late father's shadow.
We were adrift, caught in the shallows,
and Tom lambasted us with caustic wit
and legal acumen, delivering hits
with a seductive smile. There he was
waving copies of some dubious
cheques that he alleged had been signed
by some hon. members on my side,

trumpeting 'Corruption!' 'Bribery!'
With Tom's persuasive ability
such claims took root in voters' minds.
Had we stopped listening to what binds
a people to the government?
Had the fifteen years we'd spent
seeding the dream of nationhood
grown such unnutritious food?

4.
The day after our loss, I felt no grief.
To be honest, I felt some relief
as, demobbed, I pushed my cart down
a supermarket aisle. Then to town,
to Cheapside market, driving past
St. Mary's, by the church's wall
where the merciful shade from tall
flamboyants and mahoganies
protects from city's burning skies.
A balding snow-cone vendor waved
and, grinning broadly, shouted
my familiar name, 'Dipper!'
I waved, then saw in sartorial splendour
King Dyal biking in red suit, white bow-tie, gloves,
top hat, our Quixote, known for his love
of cricket and for the deplorable
reference to Bajans as 'black cattle'.
An old man, talking to himself, limps by.
A young woman is magically
transformed from sour pouts to smiling
mirth by calypso's wit – Shilling's
guitar and voice rise from a vendor's
stall and his hidden transistor.
Buoyant, light, I began to hum
with the minstrel's melodious strum:

'*My doggy loves your doggy.*
Your doggy loves my doggy.
And if our doggies
love each other, why can't we?'
Smiling, I recalled Federations'
arcing scattered stones.
It was Shilling and other griots
who'd keep alive that crucial hope
for islands drifting on our sea:
if dogs could love each other, so could we.
Knowing I'd tried to serve the people
gave me ease, left me feeling full.
Then midway through selecting fruits
brute pain lanced my right leg, a cut
that wouldn't heal. Was my body
punishing me? I headed west
to 'Kampala'. There was a mist
coming off the sea near Highway One.
The children were grown. The wife gone.
I thought 'You're on your own again.'
I watch three fishermen cast a seine
from a moses; try to forget my pain.
Brown butterflies circle a lantana
bush when I pull up at 'Kampala'.
Although it was day, the air
seemed full with the perfumed stir
of ylang-ylang, my body
its needy bottle. Silence escorted me
up the purple-heart steps. I'd make
pumpkin fritters and spinach cakes.

CHAPTER FOURTEEN

A sabbatical at Yale. Observed
a Philippine election. Chaired
a meeting in Havana for Fidel.
Built an auditorium for my people.
Fought five local elections. Kept Duffus
at bay. Even with all the fuss
over my alleged amnesia,
nothing emerged from that drama.

Grantley's siblings in history's hour,
Tom and I, but our visions of power
didn't connect. Tom, I thought, was
a puppet of the planter-merchant class
who seemed bent on taking us back
to the days when a planter claque
kept Barbados safe for privilege
and uppity blacks in bondage.
He banned journalist Rickey Singh,
ordered the regular searching
of Lamming's mail. Silenced any
calysonian or journalist who dared to pen
grievances against his party.
Every year he'd ban Gabby.

Now the hawk of corporate power
preyed on the land. A few Blacks were
allowed to rise to middling positions
in manufacturing, tourism,
banking and finance, creating
a new intermediate grouping
between the Whites and the masses
a wedge between the heights and terraces
and those in tenantries and villages.
This group, drunk with the spoils

of wealth, gated behind high walls
where dobermans and alsations prowl,
followed their former masters' old
practice of keeping jobs and contracts
sewn up in tight unspoken pacts
of family and friends; deaf to any critic
who could be labelled communistic.
I, Grantley's fourth self, saw it all:
invasions of privacy, unlawful
detentions, cover-ups of white-
collar fraud, drug-peddling, the termite
of white powder that undermined
the villages where poverty sidelined
our youth, drove them to desperate
solutions. I was known to love to fete,
to taste the pleasures of the bed
away from home; but this age bred
vices that devoured the island's health,
now cesspit for the few's unfettered wealth.

But now when Tom suddenly died,
two years after letting the U.S. hide
supplies and weapons at our airport
to invade Grenada, I played hurt,
buried my conscience to placate
Bajan sentiments, went to the State
funeral in full regalia,
performed sorrowful behaviour.
I wouldn't make the same mistake –
as over Grantley – when for pride's sake
I'd been covered in opprobrium.

Next week, at The Auditorium,
a local poet named Kellman
summed up my mood in a poem
'Conversation With a Dead Politician.'

I'd bought a copy of his book
at the door and, as he spoke,
I silently read along with him,
words darting like sprats in my mind.

'*The shadow of the sun followed the sun.*
Then you, the shadow broke at the seams
and the maggots sexed in peace.
Behind your inherited beaming wit,
a seed of darkness glinted (the spoilt child's dance)
when we turned you on, entranced
in our living rooms on Budget Day,
your reeded voice smooth and low as any Smirnoff ad.
We smelt your Machiavelli through the screen!
Your heart danced on your tongue!
Through your eyes, it shone!

Our love was a land gulping every inch of water,
and when the seam broke, when the cocaine crawled
across the island's screen, the c.i.a projected
your image on our minds, and we wanted to stare away
because your father, old Sir Grantley, was such a good man.
An ox was strapped to everyone's tongue like a sealed slap:
the journalists, the police, the Opposition.
Your Syrian friend Mr. Juman charged for possession.
Oh the fever broke but only to rise higher. The police rasped,
'Oh me hand tied. Me hands tied. Oh me hands tied up.'

Next week, Genevieve whose hand you took on British soil
did something she had never done before: after lunch
she unfurled her silent demure beauty toward the city to shop
while, alone, you fell to the bathroom floor,
sprawled on your back,
clutching your prized album of stamps.
No autopsy. No investigation.

A low-spirited nation tortured its face into a smile. Disgrace.
I didn't hear one palm tree mourn.
Just people in shock, a collective groan.
Did you?.... Did the c.i.a.
infiltrate one unassuming day?....
Did a vengeful competitor?....
Did Castro, remembering Grenada?....
Did a jealous aggrieved lover?....
Did Genevieve?....'

Tom **had** caused our country loss
by sucking-up to offshore interests,
building the phallic missiles of the banks
while we had joined the beggar's ranks –
mothers used as beasts of burden
cutting and carting sugar cane.
Where had the pride gone from our coat
of arms? We had come to connote
the prostitution of a nation
to the dollar of white tourism.
Our youth had good reason for flight.
Why stay for one more hungry night,
slap tar without the chance of work
if you were one without the right
connections. I too could have fled,
though not for want of daily bread,
but from watching my country's pain.
Like bird's wings flapping in my brain
I heard again a poet's words.
Bajans fleeing north, O my black birds,
won't you come back? Domestics catching
your tails in northern winters, scrubbing
foreign floors, running foreign elevators,
driving foreign taxis, working in foreign stores,
bring us back your rich potential
now crusted in snow. All isn't well

here on this rock, but if you will
struggle, why not do it on *your* soil?
Why such rummaging self-doubt,
such self-scathing wanderings-about?

So I rejoined the political race
and stirred, geared myself to face
the gruelling campaign ahead,
despite the things my doctors' said:
kidneys blocked by faulty ureters,
poor circulation of blood; toes
cold and dead, so with each step I took,
a dull pain spread through nerve roots
to another limb. Ignoring pain,
I led us to a huge election win.

I knew my time was ebbing fast
like island light at dusk.
In Miami the doctors shook
their heads, put me on dialysis.
I thanked them for doing their best,
went home. Eric Williams' words pressed
in on me:

> '*The enemy is not the submarine.*
> *The enemy is poverty,*
> *the enemy is suppression*
> *of the talents of our population.*'

We had pledged great social schemes
for the people. Yet, where the dream
of economic justice? Not in sight!
Real power still in the hands of Whites
averse to sharing. I knew unless
this inequity was redressed
I'd failed. White fall-out? Could I risk it?

And were the people ready for it?
Meanwhile, at the U.S. Embassy
Blacks still queue to leave the country.

Now back again at 'Kampala',
passing each canopied sash window
strengthened against storm and hurricane,
I circle the timber house that long sustained
my days; behind I hear banana trees
rustling in the light sea breeze;
loop back to the porch of purple-heart,
and as I began the slow mount
up the steps, I thought I saw the sea.
But only partially. Only partially.

Over insistent surf calling my name,
the ochre sun still brightly shone.
Sandwiched by these two eternities,
I hold my face up to the breeze,
see the sun, without forewarning,
collapse onto the sea. Sighing,
its bronze face glows with laughter,
then dissolves in circles of blue water
like ashes sprinkled from an aircraft
flying low above the Caribbean surf.

PART THREE

CHAPTER FIFTEEN

1

Early so, when all are getting up
to conches' alarms or crowing cocks,
when sun-splash ignites earth near the rocks
of bright Brandon, over-bathes a foot

of brown coral, wearied, Livingston,
a vine curling outward, yawns; then,
wrenching morning wide open,
rolls from bed with a dejected groan.

Then, face held out towards the all-
consuming holy brilliance
of the sky, this day's defiance
of failure made its morning call.

Dazzled by the glare, Livingston
squints, sees light arcing, moving in.
He thinks: *What's your meaning, brightening
light, this windless freckled morn?*

Last night at the club, scatting for
tips, few heard beyond his rhythmic
strum, his bitterly ironic
hint at imminent departure:

Island, island, full of light,
your blazing days, your blood-warm nights
will be mine until I go.
Love you so much, love you so.

How to live here? Or how to leave?
He's like one locked inside a maze
seeking an exit from these days,
stuck like a crab in the fish-net's weave.

He'd be glad to, sad to go.
But could he show these his people
a pathway from their provincial
little England? Would they ever know

that latent within their many selves
lay a deeper nation, rising
like layered coral reefs or plumbing
depths like hidden limestone caves.

So though rum-soaked tourists
loudly cheered his Creole style,
missing the irony, meanwhile,
his people laughingly dismissed

his goals, or didn't give a toss,
spiteful watchers for a hoped-for fall.
They'd hold their bellies tight and bawl:
'De fool doan know dis is Buhbados?'

So, each earnest, would-be original
thinker was crushed-up like a fool,
upstart ideas exposed to ridicule.
They'd cut him up, laugh their bellyful.

He clung to music, his last hope;
wasted it seems his English Lit. degree,
since other kinds of opportunities
for work had crumbled like burnt rope.

He found he couldn't learn the skill
of brown-nosing, fearing if one
lackeyed all day it would chameleon
one's true self away and that would kill

every artery of truth to self.
The jobs he sought – predictably –
were kept for kin of the Party-
in-Power, or sons of paler wealth.

Was it simply naivete to think
he could succeed on talent's tune?
Was he working in a vacuum?
Should he damn his pride and shrink

ambition? But the melodies
he treasured – folk, pop, kaiso –
clung tightly to him, won't let go.
They're his comforting lullabies

when light beacons from squatting chattels
as dusk falls and spreads its widening
arms across each life, and day's dins,
sun-weakened, are now weary quarrels.

Now, framed in chattel window, he
gazes across the Sunday street
to Birds River, the volleying bark
of brown mongrels crossing noisily

into the wide green pasture where
Black-belly sheep in relish graze,
munch Guinea-grass in stolid bliss,
each head in time, each jaw in metre.

Again he recalls the day the sea
sucked his father into the tides
beyond the reefs. Alone, he died.
He'd been swimming with the family

whom he chauffeured. Old Livingston
would have battled till his strength
was taken and the starved sea's mouth
swallowed him. It was in June,

birth month, the year his fifty-seventh;
his last glimpse: the east coast cliffs,
abrupt, blunt; clustering maypoles;
mile-trees' soft fannings to heaven.

The son wept with renewed grief,
and back-dragging guilt broke like a wave.
Once, he'd declared his dad a slave,
sycophant to the rich white chief.

Later, he saw such work had been
for him an open space through which he
glided, always himself, endlessly
moving as sharks circle the ocean.

Now, when sunlight ignites the dawn,
endurance is the wisdom Livvy
contemplates, a patience finely
tilled, strength he wishes he could learn,

how his dad, forced to leave school when *his* dad
took off, found odd-jobs, learnt to survive
when an uncle taught him how to drive.
If Dad slaved, he'd slaved for his child.

He'd found and lost a rare jewel
that June day when he brought
Dad's burial clothes to the Mount,
ferns for the casket, an orchid for his lapel.

As a high, brave casuarina, he'd recall
his father, keep in memory
the casket as a stone to live by;
the orchid, ferns – he'd remember all:

the white coffin gently lowered
at Westbury after Anglican
hymns and the sobbing of women;
while the squawks of a blackbird

arced in sorrow from a beam
across the zygomatic porch
as pall bearers, leaders of the church,
and friends, bore the casket all gleam-

ing white, an ironic symbol
of whence Dad's main subsistence came
that brought him, in life, a modest gain:
the patronage of white people.

CHAPTER SIXTEEN

1
Manhood weighed down young Livingston.
He grieved deeply for his mother,
too, knowing, though burdened, her
stoic, self-denying strength;

how she bore all things silently,
to not worry those around her,
though her blood pressure rose higher,
as she took pain's smart so bravely.

Good health, he knew, was draining from
her limbs – diabetes, cataract.
His will fired for her, he would wrap
the earth with sound and so bring home

a fatted rooster! Now, this morning,
turning from the window, he spots
balled-up twenty-dollar notes,
crinkled tokens of his yearning.

So he had two reasons to pursue
his quest: one was purely artistic;
the other cash. No dusty scholastic
goals for him, no bookish view.

But how to marry art and commerce
without bruising either? Could he
find a form to help him purify
the deep wound of his history's curse?

He watched some squawking blackbirds fly
from the mango's branches into the sun.
One drifted low, found seating on
his sill, held him with unblinking eye.

He saw the sky turn grey; a splash
of rain like steel pan playing low.
Cars and buses start their morning roar,
gnawing on the bubbling asphalt.

The sun returned as suddenly.
Blackbird sipped from the sill's cup
formed from chipped cement, looked up,
spread his wings and brusquely flew away.

With thoughts gathered like omens, he
sees his face in his room's hung glass,
and wonders can it come to pass
as the postered stars gaze on: Marley...

At the pine dining table his father
made, his mom had smiled and said,
'I go sleep... not feeling at all good.
I think, come morning, I'll feel better,

but when I hearing the cockcrow,
ah can hardly lift my weight to rise.
Then I forced to realize
your old mother just getting ol'.'

Mom's once-solid, deep dark frame
now spoke loudly of her frailty.
He bent, pressed four notes in her shaky
hand, hugged her, burning with love's flame,

turned his face away. Afterwards,
he roughly cranked up the old Suzuki
his dad left them, and they drove to the
clinic, leaving her in the 'death' wards

where she'd spend three long hours for new
pills to ease her pain. Livingston
had come back, gone to his room,
clasped his guitar, played a melancholy tune.

2.
Next day, more practice by the window.
A soursop, ripe, spiked udder, groans
and sways, a steady metronome
for young Livingston to follow.

Band of crows carve darkest lines
that stitch the sky like music staves.
Livvy picks out the tune they've
left. Each note, each breath contains

melodies of the heaving surf,
churning sand, and emboldened sun
that melts, destroys, restores, runs
or lies still on the barnacled earth.

He hears a knock at the door. Yes,
his girl, Dayna's come. She parks her
her bike by the porch. His feelings stir
to see her in her yellow sundress.

Mom opens up, spreads maternal
arms. They hug as if they're one blood –
'How you?'
          'Fine, Mums.' – with the love that floods
from kin. Dayna asks after all

Mums' problems, her ferns, her cannas;
Mums asking after Dayna's folk
in Rochester, her mum's consul work,
if her father's health was better.

Mums brings mauby, home-made yellow
fish cakes. Then into his room Dayna
comes, her brown hair set aflame in
the rush of light through the window...

Troubles start fading in his head.
He hears again Saturday's sounds,
wants to tell Dayna, who understands
him — mood-swings and all — what passed.

How that night, clutching his guitar,
strumming ballads he'd descended
Elena's long plush carpeted
stairs for the final set in the bar.

Swedish-mothered, Elena,
now a denizen of sweltering heat,
loved the worldly pop elite —
Clapton, Elton, Sting, Diana —

had a soft spot for this young singer,
when, boldly, Livvy sang each night:
Touch my chords, yeah light the night
with your honey words. If I never

love again, this'll be enough,
O palm-ringed naked earth receive
our love. Listeners' hands are a weave
of warm applause in steady flow.

Blue neon lights pulse on the ceil-
ings, wink on walls as bold as doves
amid spilled corn; Livvy's eyes rove
the room to check that this is real.

As the session ends his heart races
with hope. Stars glisten in his eyes;
a photo op when the lights rise;
time to take in the approving faces.

From the stockbrokers briefly put on hold;
Bajan-Yankees with their back-home cheer;
retired Britons flying everywhere
there's sun, fleeing England's constant cold;

from the newlyweds from Baton Rouge;
the Mid-West teacher with his sunburned friend,
the would-be hip, alert to every trend;
that night the audience response is huge.

As the crowd clamours for yet more,
young Livvy's heart's a brimming cup;
he notes, too, the box is filling up
with dollars. Time for an encore:

King Jaja of Opobo,
coming down to this shore.
King Jaja of Opobo,
coming down to this shore.

Down by the Wharf
when Jaja stepped off,
many Bajans came out,
and you could hear them shout:

King Jaja of Opobo,
coming down to this shore.
King Jaja of Opobo,
coming down to this shore.

And Becka tell he,
'I don't come free.
If you want to have your dream,
make me your queen.'

King Jaja of Opobo,
coming down to this shore.
King Jaja of Opobo,
coming down to this shore.

For they'd hatched a devilish plan
against one who'd driven them from Africa land.
who'd dared resist the mighty empire.
had the cheek to embarrass Victoria.

'Becka, come with me to Opobo,'
King Jaja said.
Little did he know
in two months he'd be dead.

King Jaja of Opobo,
coming down to this shore.
King Jaja of Opobo,
coming down to this shore.

*   *   *

He left Elena close to daybreak,
box clasped, headed uphill to his home;
elation drained, the stars were gone.
What new words could he find to speak

of the deep want that he hadn't done
in song? He'd defied the crass powers
that denied art, he'd sliced the lonely hours
of dark night, yet, he was still alone.

Even though he'd had his taste of fun,
though he'd smelled the perfume of the night,
he couldn't feel that things were bright.
Grief's smell still clung to Livingston:

the burden of being an only son,
the burden of supporting a widow,
the burden of feeling forced to bow
to commerce. The dead weight of living stone!

CHAPTER SEVENTEEN

1.
His boss, Noel, lumbers down the stairs
cash-till tightly clutched to narrow chest.
Bow-tie gone, his shirt undone, it's inquest
time to weigh the smoke-filled night's affairs.

To his soft-voiced six-foot guard,
he says, 'Jerry, lock up.' Heads to the bar,
relights a fat Cuban cigar,
pours a scotch and drinks down hard.

By three the patrons have all gone,
a candled Russian chandelier
casts long shadows everywhere,
but he hides his fears with cackling aplomb.

Safety's not something to regard as fun,
and Noel fears his credit's in arrears;
the creak of footfall on the stairs
could be a rival with a gun.

That night he'd won the poker game,
the takings on the drugs were high,
punters paid plenty for the pricey
girls upstairs. A visit from his tame

politician friend and life's not bad.
But elections are due and Noel's no fool,
he knows if there's a change of rule
to avoid jail he'll flee to Trinidad.

As the last staff mop the floor,
linger talking, coming down to earth,
Noel clinks another hefty scotch,
with Livingston his eyes make four.

One's cause was money, the other's art;
few words between them were spoken,
but Livvy saw a flickering token
behind Noel's suaveness of a common heart.

Noel had lived in London once,
had planned for college but opened a club,
sailed the wide channel, 'til the gate
to Sweden opened on Elena's face.

Once, Livvy had seen her laced
with smoke, heading the long table,
her low-cut gown, velvet sable,
decked with a string of pearls that graced

her slender neck. In low undertones
he heard the talk of a closed insiders' world
that twisted like the smoke and curled
in Livingston's brain. Could the tones

of his sweet guitar bring fame,
let him ride the crests of waves
to fortune's shore? Guiltily he craves
entry to their sophisticated game.

Could Noel help? Did he even know
of Livvy's dreams? What did Jerry think?
Jerry syphoned off another drink
and called his boss a gigolo

who'd wormed money from rich white women.
If the Bajan government changed
Noel'd roar like a bull deranged
and not one white queen would help him.

2.
Smiling, ready for the evening's show,
near the bar sat young Livingston
calmly tuning up *Ovation;*
Jerry came in at six or so.

Plucking notes in a ruk-a-tuk
stylee, a startled Livvy turns,
sees two men in black-grey uniforms
striding up the stairs to Noel's flat.

Jerry follows, soon comes down,
pours himself a rum and coke.
Leaning on the counter top, he looks
troubled, scowling with concern.

Lawmen, armed with batons hanging grim,
hold Noel in a painful grip;
lest he should run and give the slip
they cuff a blow or two on him.

Noel keeps cool, taking all that rain
of licks, urbane self still so sure
as they prod him roughly out the door.
Livvy thinks: *We won't meet again.*

Packing up his guitar, he heard
Jerry's laboured breath, his fear
rattling around the awestruck bar.
'O God! Mister Noel...' Jerry paused,

'Mister Noel get deport!
All we go dead!' The barman capped
the *Cockspur*, wonders what could be tapped
to sell; for what he could be bought.

Livvy did not stare in quite such horror.
Just that morning came the news:
Noel's clout had healed his blues –
a contract at London's *Troubadour*!

Noel, then, had known his heart,
seen displayed his bright desire,
grasped his singing's urgent tone (or
heard him sigh between each set).

Here was bittersweet irony –
Livvy promised he'd truly write it down,
catch life's fragility in song –
that Noel, falling to his knees,

had used his dwindling influence
to get the key he needed for his flight.
His thoughts rustled gladly through the night:
how one flew over the other's descent.

CHAPTER EIGHTEEN

1.
'Go, go get your dreams, my darlin' son,
Go get your dreams. Don't you worry
'bout me. Church yout's does come by,
and your uncles, Donald and Allan.

Her words couched like some great pelican.
offering nurture to its young.
On the porch wall, where sunlight sung
the joy of morning, for Livingston

humped intense, between elation
and guilt, his arms wrapping his knees,
her words seemed brightening bells
of pentecostal benediction,

but he guessed her sorrow's pain despite
her smiles. This and the taste of bush tea
he was sipping were the memories
he'll carry with him on the BA flight

that would leave Barbados behind.
She'd miss him greatly, that he knew,
but he saw dolphins arcing the blue
Atlantic, the call of fame razoring his mind.

2.
Heathrow's air was crisp but yet
so sunny, never suggesting
the onslaught of winter's cold knifing
through his thin woollen overcoat.

A tall, toothy man with rubicund
cheeks was holding up a cardboard sign
printed in caps with Livvy's name.
Waving the sign, he stood behind

the Customs desk. Livvy saw it
and waved back, but soon had to beckon him
to come forward. There was a problem
with his papers: no work permit.

Toothy man comes to customs point.
Livvy's Bajan passport exit stamp
not proper. Livvy sees the creep
of fingers flexing at the joint,

poised to stamp on his quailing heart:
No admittance, when in cool style
the toothy man proffers a pile
of papers that seem to fit the part.

He said Livvy was a big rock star
here to collect his royalties.
Practised charms were scuttling fast as
spiders over toothy man's jaw.

He said Livvy's permit, overdue,
would be ready in a few days.
With a non-work permit he could stay
for six days. Livvy was sent through.

Andrew Mayers said, 'Close!' Then took
up one of Livvy's carry-ons.
'Close call. Welcome, old son, to England.'
Livvy saw he had one limping foot.

When they reached the baggage claim,
hauled his luggage from the carousel,
Andrew said: 'What happened to Noel
was bad. Stunned me. What a crying shame!

Real nice chap. I'd known 'im for years.
Someone put a mean frame-up on 'im.
He spoke well of you, real good things.
He sent us once a tape of yours...

Good Friday set... recorded that day...
Really good.' They soon drew near
Mayers' Vauxhall, an old two-door.
'I look forward to hearing you play.'

Wrapped in this new-place happiness,
Young Livvy sniffed its strange aromas,
like the motheaten books at home,
lofty Tennyson's ballads pressed

next to the epic song of Homer –
remedy for the traveller's
self-doubt – a wealthy family's
gifts given to their loyal brown driver.

He watched strangers huddling on
the streets, looking inward yet from
self's loneliness being drawn –
all the ironies of attraction.

He heard starlings smugly twittering
on the limes. Soon, the *Troubadour's*
in view. Cavernous and cold, its bare
basement flat was his lodging.

Black coffee – an old maid's angelus –
became his morning's redemption.
In Hyde Park, or here, he pencilled songs
that'd make rainbows weep, or the one last

programmed lemming cut its date with death.
His songs shaped in a Creole style
(Euro-African folk) battle
aloneness with its frosty breath.

He'd show how vocal force and rhythmic strength,
profound lyrics and pure melodies
could work as one. Still, painfully,
aloneness wrapped him with frosty breath.

He'd build his voice with Ms. Lockhart,
tighten up his craft. Once a week
for two hours in her rooms they'd meet.
Always perky, his tutor would start

with deep breathing for strength and control
in mid, upper, and lower lungs. Next,
he'd prop chest with thumbs, index
touching index, then a slow pull-

ing out like an accordion's bellows
with each deep inhale, returning
step by step to join them again
when he exhaled. Ten minutes for

those reps. Felt like water's flow to
open inner spaces... and then
keyboard scales like arcing islands
sending their free light upward to

heaven. 'Sing the vowel. Sing it loud.
Hold, hold the 'Uh' in 'sun' until
your breath runs out.... Ready?' What a thrill
of light-headedness, vertiginous

high cliff. He followed her long range.
She went alto, lower and lower,
then higher, up and down. With her
help he built up to three-octaves.

He learnt slowly how to slip inside
his 'head' voice, with ease ascending
to high registers, then returning
to normal voice and Lockhart's breezy smile.

3.
Those first weeks he thought much of Dayna,
how they'd met at the club one night
and after casing his guitar, the sight
of her had dazzled the Elena.

She beamed on top the slenderest
frame. 'I love your music,' she
said smiling. 'So original, so free.'
'Thank you. Thanks for your comment.'

Livvy pursued, promised he'd call
(*and* real soon) the number that she gave.
Their one rhythm sparked with the agave's
yellow stars where sea cranes mull

with love. One year, almost to that day,
she'd found Bimshire after undergrad.
Her mum's peace-corpsed sojourn gave the nod
to stretch self, engage with other space.

Laughter had always filled their hours,
but her letter was full of sorrow.
She was leaving for New York to go
to share her dying dad's last days.

Livvy reached for pen and paper,
shifted near the shadeless basement
bulb that lit a circle always dim;
wrote, 'Ready to love again', for her.

Like a cloudy sky touched by the sun
I get warm by the light in your eyes.
Every old shadow just fades away
when I see the brightness of your smile.

I gaze across green open fields
where a thousand butterflies dance.
But none can take away the blues like you.
I'm so glad for another chance.

I'm ready to love again,
to feel the sweet exchange,
and of all the things I know,
I'm ready to love again.

I hope these feelings never end,
and our love will only grow.
Two fields, a sun, a cloudless sky —
there's so much more to know.

Of all the loves I've had,
with you, baby, it's never felt so right.
I'm weary of the past, had enough of that.
I'm living on, loving on in your light.

Oh I'm ready to love again,
to feel the sweet exchange;
and of all the things I know,
I'm ready to love again.
I'm ready to love again.
Let's love again.

The song relieved yet saddened him.
Making art from experience
was art's freeing gift, jubilance
and song's sorrow, those crazed jealous twins.

He missed Dayna's dimpled loveliness,
but wrote only sparsely, off-and-on.
He'd sent postcards telling how he'd won
a contract and such news. Far from her kiss,

songs subbed for woman. Loneliness
now stemmed more painfully from a heart
split with loss of love. Soon, once-saving art
seemed enemy. Perhaps, he'd caressed,

too intently, this strange soil?
He longed to glove success and to glow.
At each aching sunset, at each night's show,
he poured himself out like rarest oil.

But without knowing, his first love,
coral-flavoured, fell from favour;
the creole tunes lost their savour,
fled like fleeting clouds from the rough

gust of new wind. Mum had gaily blessed
him that morning of departure.
He must succeed, if only for her.
So, while he yearned for the sparkling crest

149

of waves, morning's cock-crows, the long palms'
rattling rhyme, this seemed dream; the fact
was promise of a record contract.
How to marry Art and Mammon?

At Star Music, he paid ninety-pounds
for some demo tracks. Then, trembling
with dread, mailed them to Palm Records. In
a room tense with hope, Chris said: 'Your songs

quite good, man, 'speci'ly the lyrics.
But you need some stronger hooks.
Just keep working hard, man, 'cause it looks
like you'll soon get there. Keep at it.'

Truth? Polite rejection? Sound
advice? Giving himself the one-year
contract's length, he'd boldly wear
his music like a robe, like a crown.

4.
He could see Mums' right hand shook
the words out. Concern for him was
in that hand. As seen through frosted glass,
a quivering letter moved its foot.

His ambition (supporting his mum,
and finding meaning through music),
was a pounding wind at his back,
a loud and sombre drum.

Chris's words echoed like sea shells
from other well-meaning mouths.
Where was now the summons of the conch?
A distant fading, a dying knell.

His Creole residue, he feels
was holding him back; it was now
a drag, tiring him like a sea-sloughed
swimmer under scowling swells.

Now he'd change tack. If he let recede
his island past, fully give himself
to English-flavoured styles and themes,
he'd make it. Thus focused, he'd succeed!

Just a pause, a tactical detour,
till he gained shore. So Livingston
stripped all coral, stopped writing home.
London became his writing's core.

A live mind that's emptying of old thoughts
attracts new ones. Now, in reverse,
he felt stresses shifting from the first
and third to the second and fourth.

A small label liked him, so they pressed
a two-track chart single. He had passed
one test, affirmed his goal, and cashed
a modest profit. But in his head

were murmurs of plants, animals
that should mean nothing to him any more.
Oblique, unclear – he tried to ignore
the rustling of their teasing calls.

CHAPTER NINETEEN

1.
Donald's letter came with grey dust-
toned smell, bringing rain clouds in April,
the wind sweeping over in a squall;
umbrellas spreading like jumbie mush-

rooms. Read and reread with its death
smell that grey morning in April:
'...*tablets taken; a little*
inside sleep, she sip she final breath.

'*She just went to sleep so and don't*
get up. Dah, son, is de best way
to go'. Stricken, hounded by this day,
the son clasped his guitar for comfort.

The grave's call, sun-surfed, assailed him here.
Hard on his heels, it followed his tracks;
it squatted cat-still at his back;
he burned inside with a primeval fear.

A sparrow's cold eye gave reproof:
stranger too long on London's streets.
The cold grey roads refuse his feet;
he's pressed down by the cold grey roofs.

Livvy wrote of his sure intent
to come home for mother's funeral,
but ambition and guilt began to tussle
as he tossed and turned in the cold basement.

He was betraying his mum in death, but fear
he would dim those starry neon lights
held him back from coffined rites.
Yet, her love still touched him here.

As guilt's bayonet nudged him down
Old Brompton's gusty streets, he knew
that for his life he had to go
from London's dreams, return to home.

He'd touch Mum's grave and then come back;
confront the stalking shadows cast
by island headstone. But so much was
at risk. Would he lose his contract?

And sole child, once there, the funereal
demands, the grief of relatives,
might take more time than he could give,
might put his career hopes in thrall.

How would his manager reply?
Sympathy for his fellow man?
Or practised not to give a damn
who dead, dying; who laugh or cry?

Armed with this firm intent, he'd go:
those breezes that had brought tidings
of death, would hurl him back quick time.
Brevity would be his motto.

2.
A late May snowfall; Heathrow's like
a Chekov scene. A taut face boards
the craft, looks down as the plane soars,
sees London vanish, feels airsick

and fearful leaving all this behind.
Bare oaks, lawns carpeted with snow,
mere specks of pattern down below
as Livingston drifts mistlike in his mind.

It's Easter and he hears once more
his father's mellow baritone
singing the Pascal hymns that are blown
across Deacons Primary pasture.

He's in his angst-filled thirteenth year,
flying a kite that bobs and lifts,
fearful the wind might drop and twist
it tumbling earthward; or that it might soar

so high it couldn't hold the strain.
The skeleton would break its spine
of dried sugar fronds, and the twine,
though waxed, would from the kite unchain.

Then indeed, the angel's spine, pawed
by strong winds, broke and his kite's ribs
collapsed, torn cloth flapping like lips
of fear round the trembling, straining cord.

Soon that lifeline snapped, and he sped
beneath the angel's wings past Rick's Sports
Club (where many wayward boys
were tamed). Wings flapped over the tar bed

at Spring Gardens. Lost beyond the trees,
the poor angel vanished. Livingston
crossed the highway to the beach, sand
warm between his toes. On his knees,

breathless, he stares beyond the sea's
cargo: men and women chatting;
swimmers' bobbing and ducking
heads in swelling tides; merry screams

and splashes, brawling and youthful;
intense joggers; tourists who chose
here, yet wear a coy smile and the pose
of those who can never be too careful.

Beyond these noisy hordes, near a yacht,
a sinking redness brightly flashed.
Livvy leapt and cut a path splash-
ing through resisting water. He fought

the sea, fought like it'd done everything
to cause his galling grief; he gave
his all to reach the watery grave,
dived deep to where his kite was sinking,

emerged gasping with its torn cloth
stained by sea's salt, the red-yellow
strips now a dripping crude banner.
He wept. Would it fly again? Who knows?

That loss, grating, was only one dearth.
He wept harder, perhaps, for the speed
of it all; how angels, too, could bleed,
were not immune from common death.

Powerlessness was what he couldn't deal
with as he'd tried to save the kite
from drowning, as he'd lost the fight
to save his heavenward soaring angel.

So he raged against what he'd seen
of flesh-weakness against immortal
water: grim god that can pull
all things downward: old shoes, strewn

lover's clothes, bottles, kites… and fathers…
his mind reminded with a jolt,
but found relief from grief's assault
to find his plane still in the air.

3.
He wasn't ready for return's shock,
how new, sudden, the warm island air,
how strangely people spoke. Not yet a year,
he'd lost much of his coral talk.

He first heard it near the Customs point.
Ears strained and cringed below home's
tongue. To his horror, Livingston
felt a stranger, out of joint.

A slow-moving cabman greeted him,
took his bags and fired the car.
Guilt cursing his first departure,
could Livvy reconnect to Bim?

Like fireflies, cars were zipping by,
the night air a warm enclosing
hand, but tenseness was winnowing
him. Maybe to find seed he'd try

to get his feelings down. He asked
the cabman for some light just when
he saw the little house left to him,
(for a fee its care a neighbour's task).

The ballpoint had first formed this return:
mother's death, that shattering
breach of blood; the ever sobering
thought that death would no one spurn.

The bridge then led him up a stranger
path that went beyond the sphere
of being earthbound, literal.
He would call the song, "Another

Night". In it a lover loses
his woman while away at work,
returns, mind tight with hope and hurt.
Fireflies. Perfume. Almond eyes.

I came back to limestone, to the rock where I was born.
Two fireflies above me led the taxi to my home.
The house was in darkness; I turned on the light.
The room glowed around me, took me back to another night.

Saw the couch we sat on, smelt her perfume everywhere.
Eyes like almonds, flowers in her hair.
She's somewhere better now, my comforters said.
Still I long to touch her, feel her fingers on my head.

And yes, I remember that rainy night in September
when we walked into this room, walked into this room.
And yes, I remember we were so young and tender
when we walked into this room, oh we walked into this room.

I came back to limestone, to the rock where I was born.
Two fireflies above me led the taxi to my home.
The house was in darkness. I turned on the light.
The room glowed around me; took me back to another night.

Dayna. Dayna. Would he ever
feel again her spirit's sweet caress?
Riding home to emptiness,
was the Atlantic ever wider?

Stone melodies began to surge and race
with the immensity of the sea.
The cabman was staring at Livvy,
at the tears running down his face.

4.
Next day, surrounded by Sharon's
sunstruck evergreens and the churchyard's
rattling flamboyants, Livvy heard
in a climbing truck's laboured groan

a supplicant's call for forgiveness.
Under the sun's leavening heat,
thawing out the cold round his heart
at the grave-side fleshed with guinea grass,

he stood still and heard absolution
humming. From the trees pentacostaling
leaves a woman's soft voice sung,
"You had tongue but didn't keep you head on.

Your green heart just leap so to embrace
the strange. Listen again to de wind-
blown palms talking, de sea salty lines.
Dem should be you guide, you true face."

5
Her words roused in him buried voices
of plants, animals; green shoots of new
music forming as their sounds grew
clearer, swelling with choices.

Next day, tuning in his radio,
with a convert's zeal Livvy felt betrayed
when a Tuk tune was named by a deejay
as Ring Bang, all the worse, moreso

as the man basked loudly in that theft,
as if giving name to the crime
made it legitimate. It was time
to re-engage with coral's gift.

He dressed quickly, bound for Elena,
slapping tar down steep Bishop's Hill,
past the two blood-red flame trees that filled
the exultant sky with splendour.

Steaming asphalt fierce as guilt,
a rankling bitter underscore
erupting like a deep buried sore
into the healing of pure island light.

He reached Elena's driveway – cracked
with huge pot-holes and full of litter.
Shards of broken bottles glitter
in the sun. Livvy stopped and looked.

Tall shrubs and trees were all he saw.
The building had disappeared. Not
a brick, nothing. He saw, on the hot
shore of memory, the wall-

to-wall carpet; Noel's urbane
frame being prodded down the stairs;
the glowing Russian chandeliers
casting light on Dayna's name;

her dimpled cheeks, her kind compliments;
her sure living in her self; his long
flight from self, his desertion
of stone for modest success. Regrets.

CHAPTER TWENTY

1.
In the vexed wind rushing through palms'
ribs he hears the hounding howl
of the furies trailing the foul
blood-crime of his leaving; to the psalm

of the pounding sea – its salty soup
the seabirds' one everlasting course –
his guilt-chords vibrate with the force
of threshing angels' wings. In a loop:

half-here, half elsewhere, Livvy's lost
in the dark night of his spirit's
kyrie, shamed by the sea-spray's spit
as he lunges along the coast,

eyes downcast on the rejecting sand.
How find the words, the way to span
the gulf, find some healing hyphen
to rejoin dragging past to the hand

of the impatient leading future?
Livvy's so deeply sunk in thought
he cannot hear the true import
of the soft breezes that whisper

in his ears, or see the flocks of birds
round the man sauntering up the beach.
The fisherman waits till Livvy reach,
then lowers the net of his words.

'Here, hold that shorter side fo' me.'
The long end he hoisted out the moses.
They shook dried leaves and many mosses
on sand's mat, and what they could not free

this way were removed by hand.
Man's skin, purest ebony;
torso straight: a grand palm tree.
'I see you hey evuh day, my man.

But doan tek life suh hard. Things'll work out.
I patch *Lady Ann* for two days now.
Boat cyan sail wid holey prow.
When I done, I spread me mout'

and t'ank mighty Jesus. Life that way.
Yuh got hills and valleys, sea and sun,
so yuh tek um, just so, as it come
and trust tomorrow's a better day.'

Livvy feels the words enter
his mind, heart. He asks, 'Who you name?'
Smiling, sea-man said, 'Sea Crane
is wha' people call me since I's four.

De name stick firm like gum on me knees.
And you?'
            'Name is Livvy Codrington.'
'Dah good. Livvy stand for Living Stone,
also Tamer of the Seas.

Hold you shape, absorb de light,
reflect goodness to everyone.
Dah is how you's wake up, Son.
How you hold you favoured heat.'

Livvy sees movement, his eye runs
to a young woman walking alone.
Turns back; blinks: fisherman gone.
A crane bores its pathway to the sun.

Would Sea Crane return so he could mount
his wide wingspan, comb the azure heights?
How long for a glance of sunlight
beyond world's dark, keening mouth?

For five weeks, he kept angelus.
Each day Sea Crane would tell him something
new – ancient truths that made to sing
in him all things native, and enough

to firm-up his stumbling limbo
dance. Now Time says no more delay,
time to make steps to seize the day;
time to risk grimmest inferno

of humiliating fall, to free
stiff back, bend backwards in the dance
of freedom's complex balance
towards Divinest comedy.

He looks into the shadows of
a world he has not made but is
the only one he can influence with his
actions. He sees the cargoes of

his foreparents arrive, their terror
of fixed exile; but then to see
them leap like shoals of fish in gaiety,
nuances the absolutes of horror.

He sees them welcome the passing
of each Act that promises to unlock
their hopes, but how like submerged rocks
deep fears belie the glory day's rejoicing.

2.
Livvy's walking seaward was
daily ritual, gesture of a fool
to pride's high jaw. But no ridicule
(though his car-borne schoolmates paused

with snide courtesy or sheer pity
for his lonely asphalt-slapping fate)
could block growing vision, nor take
from him talking palms or singing sea.

Surf-drawn, he passed an old woman
framed in a louvred window that
overlooked the seaside street. What
her name was he never knew, but, some-

times he'd stop and they would talk
(sunlight catching the croton hedges
and cars screeching hard as if it is
Rally Day). She'd eagerly speak

of her seven children who had flown
away far North. Soon, her wrinkled smile
cleaved to Livvy, her new child.
Their brief exchanges glowed like the sun.

Yet, deep within he heard piteous
groans: his own lost one. May her rest
be sweet. May the bright light of her east
warm his heart's temporal house.

3.
Each day, Sea Crane's book of truth
turned new wave-pages. Livvy ate
his words like the starved laureate
who found the home despised in youth.

He dives to the sea's emerald depth,
boring like a glinting silver fish.
That same strolling woman turns her face,
sees him pierce the surface, out of breath.

She hails him from inside a high wave's
curving lilt, Trini-Bim accent
laced with surf. The sea's naked scent
was amniotic, raw. Elbows scathe

the water, as if performing
some aqua-aerobic exercise,
water swishing up from slender thighs
to bubbly brown dougla breasts bobbing

like buoys marking depth. Fat fruit. She
stood, then sloshed shoreward, head airborne,
hair like thick love-locks or unshorn
wool, her glance a question to Livvy.

Then gazing at something further on,
pursed lips seeming to frame a whistle,
she gathers bag and wraps towel
around her waist. Then she puts on

sun glasses, straw hat, waves a hand
and heads down-beach, a burden and thrill
combined. Livingston watched her until
she was a moving dot on distant sand.

CHAPTER TWENTY-ONE

1.

That same day, standing at her window
Levinia, sea-maid, watches twilight's
warm breath flicker the village, and night
invade houses she had long known.

She thinks of what has led her here –
the years of learning at Cave Hill;
despair, flight to the States; the treadmill
of work; love lost in Georgia;

the pain when a heart turned to stone
rebels and wants to live again.
What good a life of discipline
if it leaves one sleepless and alone,

a well-thumbed *Coping With Insomnia*,
her paperback room mate. As night
passes and no sleep comes, moonlight
floods in and memory's depths are plumbed.

2.

Four years of dedicated study
at Cave Hill. Until exams were done
she'd not been one to lime or run
around for thrills – her sense of duty

well inscribed from precepts taught at home.
She'd kept the promises made to mother –
no child, no abortion, or other
hazarding of reputation.

She'd sung surf songs, though within reason;
set a heart or two afire,
played campus pageants, leads in choir,
had healthy shares of college fun.

But all agreed it looked a cert
she'd end up with at least an upper
second-class. Come September,
there'd surely be no problem finding work.

She'd held close the tales from motherland
of great-grands who fled from poverty's
sour karmic vines to the West Indies
on a salt-glazed passage of illusion;

shipped from Calcutta or Madras,
to feel the bitterness of ex-slaves
swelling, hating this new wave
who took labour from their hands;

who slaved on the plains of Caroni,
saved every cent (or rum-sucked them
in despair); then fade the dreams of return:
ragas cry over a Trini pyre.

Her parents met in Trinidad –
a church event in Saint Augustine
where choirs gathered from there and Bim –
soon wedding vows were gladly shared.

Born in Bim, her good father was
African; her Indian mother
from Trinidad, call *her* dougla,
a creole light in Barbados.

Her mother, homemaker; father was
a showroom clerk. In Cavans Lane,
he worked late for his daughter's gain.
Genuine aspiring lower class.

So after splurging on hot channa,
post-grad fetes with all her friends,
she'd concentrated on making ends
meet: work before hosanna.

She kept hunting for a position
to repay her parent's sacrifice,
help them add a room to the house,
make reality of their vision.

But closed doors. Even when, temping, she
proved herself, sure a job was hers,
someone else, through the net of favours
affluence weaves, got the booty.

Months lengthened sharp as cane-blades.
One day, strolling on Brandon's Beach,
she met Joan Ince, who used to teach
her at high school, knew her good grades,

and with an agave's single eye
saw her old student's urgent need.
Told her: 'You'd soar. You'd succeed
on the graduate programme where I

teach in Georgia. You'd get in. . .'
She took G.R.E., her scores were good.
Yet, loving home was too sweet food
to lose for the uncertainty of going.

But while desire to remain stayed strong –
she didn't want to leave, to fly
this landscape so lucid in her eye –
frustration grew the louder song.

When South-laced accents telephone
her last chance to take the fellowship,
urgency flushed each fingertip,
the decision must be hers alone.

If Bim wouldn't get her a job,
misplaced loyalty shouldn't hem her,
and trap her in frustrations gutter.
Her parents blessed her, understood.

In five weeks she'd head for Atlanta,
take a Masters in Business Admin.
Twenty-two, she was certain
it was for the best. For sure, the soca

fetes she'd miss; and the beaches,
the soft brown sand that moved like lace
between the toes, a gentle tickling grace;
the surf's fizz that would always reach

into the depth's of midnight's song.
But her future blazed with confidence,
igniting hope's heady incense,
antheming, 'Georgia, here I come!'

CHAPTER TWENTY-TWO

1.
Her head still on the deal window,
as night spreads the scent of rose blooms
over familiar homes in dark entombed,
she feels again the sharp arrow

of innocence lost one Georgia
night. Desire, wrapped in carnival
cloth had crept up in an artful
dance, groaning promises in her hair.

But before that Georgia had been new,
somewhere to discover, test for
difference: find where it gave her
space, or imposed a narrower view.

2.
When first she moaned about the heat,
she'd be told, 'Levinia,
you's full o' it. You ain't an islander?
Ain't cha?' Scarce a breezy street

in midsummer Atlanta. Concrete
towers keep out the slightest wind,
seal humid breath tight within,
imprison those whose powerless feet

once marched with King, whose exclusion
mocks Auburn's bright, everlasting flame.
But culture not race was her first pain:
culture of a provincial oven.

In creole Barbados, instinctive
style was to mix: soca, reggae, ruk-a-tuk,
chutney, samba, pop and folk...
The world's rhythms all there alive.

Here, there were no shades of grey;
here the world was either black or white,
fixed in monocultural sight.
She was charming, they would say,

but people, mostly Black,
wearing hardship's heavy badge, paint
her culture as exotic, lightweight.
That fact disturbs. She feels this pack

of closed minds can never guess its end –
black and white crabs, confused, stuck
in scowling, raging holes. But that
was their fate, not hers. She won't bend.

3.
Boldness gave her a nonchalance
that with her prominent cheekbones
seized a watcher's fancy; circling hands
round glass, he observed her in frank

discourse with some sisters at
Peachtree's Kaya, as caffeine fumes
coiled and curled around the room.
Perky, unfettered breasts mapped

the scene's presumed consent in the heat
of night. Coolly, he asked. Politely,
she turned, nodded, and soon they hit the
strobe-lit floor, snaking to the beat.

When the lights dimmed, laughing she
exchanged numbers, though she held no
hopes for meetings like this. The glow
of lights can deceive. When groggily

one woke, now sober, a new tune,
regret's melody can soon advance,
a shaming, self-despising lance,
that leaves behind a festering wound.

A man may sport a cloven hoof
which last night's scotch had nicely hid:
the devil lurks beneath what's promised.
Ask old Faust if you want some proof!

CHAPTER TWENTY-THREE

1.
He seemed different, cool, had travelled
the world. Army man, based at Augusta's
Fort Gordon, his Atlanta trip was
a homecoming. Handsome, gravel-

voiced, this man called Gregor Jones
seemed off a page of *Ebony,*
his gloss tenceled; his life, a story,
open, loving all the world.

His charm a string of shining pearls,
he courted her with easy grace,
comfortable with any class or race;
under his sun she soon unfurls.

He wore her like a buttonhole;
she flattered to be so much prized.
Now caution is to be despised,
quick marriage is their mutual goal.

2.
Driving through Fort Gordon's army base,
she gawked, quite stunned by its extent:
banks, gas stations, and theater lent
it a city's feel, with ample space

for a post office, fire station,
restaurants, and all the usual
franchises that provide consumer fuel
from East to West coast of the nation.

A golf course bordered by exclaiming pines,
acres of tennis courts far as eye can see,
a boating lake to saunter by;
the only blot: the military signs.

She gazed long, absorbing all that's new
on that muggy summer's day when
the sun bleached the world to ashen
dullness, haze fading out the view

past a water tower hovering
behind elms; past the Medical
Center, past the Leisure Travel
Exchange, Greyhounds muzzling in.

Greg's place laid out carefully as
a still-life. Careful and close detailing,
the green plates all rimmed with bordering
pine-cones, all so self-contained,

all so polished, the selfsame way...
She found a job at the high school,
teaching; shunned mall culture's rule
at weekends; indulged Saturday

morning rounds of yard sales, bouts
of boredom, which new friends (like her
mostly wives of officers)
lived for. Loved, though, the cook-outs

enthusiastically given
every month in each other's yards.
And when she got beyond their hard
brashness, how she loved these women,

bruised and brave: simplicity's
good hearts, classless and for real.
From them she learned small wounds to heal,
learned to hush pain's intensity,

laugh at self. But when, the next year
duty called Greg away to Berlin,
her own career goals were growing –
a banner urging her to declare

her resolve to stay in Augusta,
though Greg would be gone all year.
But as month followed month, her fear
grew when he hardly called her.

Once, when a friend said, 'Call him NOW!'
she was answered by a woman's
soft voice. Her spirits sank again.
'Worthless he-dog!' Friends told her how

she must think less of Greg. Older,
wiser, their advice flowed free:
'Just have yo'self some fun. Think he
ain't?' She felt the price would be for her

too great. Greg returned, then was transferred
(the blessed curse of the U.S. Army)
north to old blue-grass Kentucky.
When they spoke now, it occurred

to her, bonds had shrunk to duty;
like burnt trash in fields of sugar cane,
their love died, leaving only pain.
Then when Milosevic's cruelty

sent Greg's unit to the Balkans,
though she feared his return in a bag,
she knew their marriage was a rag
too torn to mend. She took her friends'

advice to taste wild secret sex
for the first time. Now she really felt
how loveless a time Greg had dealt
her. He would have to be her ex.

When next he showed, she told him this.
Sheepish grins soon turned to sneers,
pretend surprise at what he hears.
'How could you break our married bliss?'

She said he wouldn't have to pay,
so settlement came without dirt.
No strings, no small children to hurt.
And so they split and went their ways.

3.
Her searching for a single's flat,
led her, hopeful, to the Hill.
The phone voice, an eager squirrel
sensing a deal, replied: 'We've got

something. Come on up.' Then, a cough
as words falter in the landlord's
throat. *My accent*, *that old record.*
She thinks Africa, somewhere far-off.

She pulled into the driveway, jaws
tight with foreboding. She soon spies
through parted curtains darting eyes.
The woman rushes down to draw

a line the alien couldn't cross,
making the edges of her red brick
fortress sharp. Levinia, feeling sick,
is repelled from the woman's house.

'I'm so sorry. Really,' she began.
'Someone called before and they just
phoned back to take the flat. I must
let them have it, you understand?'

'What you really mean is that,
after all these centuries,
after science prove our genes
the same, you won't rent to a Black?'

'That's not true,' the woman said.
Levinia spun round in anger,
and shaking strode back to the car,
pleased the woman's face was red.

'You should be ashamed of yourself.
I curse all you stand for.' Away she sped,
strangely uplifted. Dust billowed
pleasingly when the car took off.

4.
Oak Lane provides a four-room flat
in what she's sure is a nice area,
a comfortable berth for her
and snuggly Lucky, her black cat.

But at the spa on Wrightsboro,
Donna, so cheery when she'd booked,
ignored her, fled, guiltily looked
away. After half an hour, she rose,

176

inquired quite calmly at the desk.
Thirty more long minutes pass. Then
a smart, fiftyish-looking man
brings the bad news. The masseuse, Jess,

just now fell ill and must go home.
His tone, like the white landlord's,
invokes the ancient Jim Crow words,
still wounding in the Southern sun.

The man knew she wouldn't return;
friends would not come. Management's
goal to stay pure achieved, to fence
their blood without 'Whites Only' signs.

She left gloomily, sat in the car
for ages. Of course, the masseuse
never left. Levinia's cheupse
near cracked the window of the spa.

That night, Holiday Inn was where
she'd take on day's despair and renew;
drinks in the happy hour, a dance or two,
maybe someone with whom to share

her hurt. A large man came, asked if he
could sit at her table. 'Sure.' Two
teeth were gold-capped. A voice with a coo,
but pleasant enough despite goatee.

She spoke of the day's encounter.
'That's Disgusta for you, girl,' he sighed.
'Once, a Jamaican friend and I
went to a joint. A hot dancer

worked her shit as long as some folks
watched. But when Frederick and I
alone sat watching there (my
God!) she quit and not a soul

told her labor laws required she work.
A pissed amputee wheeling like some weird
red ant, shouted, "You get outta here!"
That bald barman eyed us with a smirk.'

Trevor's frank story soon erased
the come-on fears Levinia
nursed when he'd first approached her;
a large man hoping for a lay?

They'd both come to purge the beast,
to trade stories of sick Disgusta,
its slow, deadly, dark nostalgia,
the dogwood beauty that hid its teeth.

Divorced, lonely, he'd called an escort
service. From his second-floor
window, sees the pimp-driven car
in the parking lot, sees the tart

get out, sassy in white cotton,
a pleasant look upon her face,
walking head-up to the staircase.
Her knock sounds, and Trevor opens

the door. Woman's exuberance goes
when she sees him. Her shoulders drop.
'I can't do it. Not with you,' she sobs.
'They'll send you someone else, you know.'

They danced, she and Trevor. Levinia,
thought: *Augusta, where even hookers*
are racist. It is no wonder
most Blacks stick to their own area,

to stop the whiplash to their hearts.
Only so long folks will reach out.
When they do, they must tout
a rock-steady mind, or fall apart.

She'd leave this Southern gothic place
before year-end. She'd best resign
before ol' Bradford screwed her mind;
back to a city too busy for race.

The mild witness of Atlanta's
racial face could not compare
to this. Ability was all it cared
for. Atlanta would be better.

But there were other voices in
her head, the sound of coral stones
all hissing, 'Lost.' Deep in her bones
she felt her limestone island calling.

CHAPTER TWENTY-FOUR

1.
Gardenias begin to bawl
in May, blooming singly first, till
fruity white rushes drape and fill
the air with scent like a knitted shawl.

In May she goes to Atlanta.
On I-20 West, her U-Hauled luggage
ruffles – drifting ship's wreckage
swept along the sea's hard shoulder.

The rear view holds a sight that fills
the heart – woman, galvanized with Spring!
A force swells in her, despair won't win.
Her eyes dig sunlight from the hills.

She sees the pines surround the islands.
Water land. Two bluebirds dip by
Echo Lake, then onward soaring fly.
Faith stretches until her eye lands

on a wooden house, its black roof
humped dark on green rolling hills
where dogwoods foam with joy. She feels,
she knows, one day she'll own one, proof

that heart's wholeness lies in homestead,
the sense of landscape's rightness here,
right now. She feels that every fear
has gone. She is alive, not dead.

She's learnt to make the venom run,
after nursing a poisoned heart.
She'll love self now, won't give a fart,
knows every wound has its reason!

2.
Each Atlanta dawn, she rose as bride
(and blessed groom); would eat a plate
of fresh baked cinnamon cup cakes,
with strawberries, coffee. She'd have lied

to say lust did not sometimes seize
her eye – lust hisses endlessly –
but no man-wish lasted. Before she
fell for another, hell would freeze.

When daily she passed Echo Lake
as it drank the ashen morning sky,
the straggling shreds of misery
fell from her, and the last dull ache

of past ghosts fled. But watching swans
gliding on the ripples in their pairs,
so faithful in their mute affairs,
who can dismiss love for all seasons?

3.
Deepest suburban Atlanta
gave her space to breathe, the privacy
to grow. Teaching math at a high
school near Ridgecrest long gave her

pleasure. But when pressed to join
the Caribbean Club she found
again an itch, a complex wound
that rankling made her pine,

stung with the tang of memory's salt
of plant, polyp, animal. Soon
island voices piled like limestone
on her dreams, her peace assault.

Each month's first Saturday the club met
at the church on Columbia Drive.
The priest, white but creolised,
had fallen in the Carib net

between World Wars when a scuffle
through the islands berthed at Kingston,
and a brown-skin girl took him in.
He stayed, slain by all things tropical.

Later he found God, wed his angel,
and only left the island when
she died, yet never lost his yen
for all the Caribbean's creole

charms. Each new member of the club
was greeted like a rediscovered friend
who brought the excuse to descend
again into memory's warm tub.

With his priest's confessional air
Levinia soon found herself
taking down from the private shelf
thoughts she felt were hard to share.

'I can't stand the limits,' she said.
'I mean... really... from a cultural
standpoint.' Seeking more, Father Moss pulled
his nose, scratched, then lowered his head.

'See me! Like plant and animal!
I want to live everywhere
at the same time. Each island's there
for real, but they'll fight 'til they're full

of self only. Crabs in separate
barrels struggling blindly in distress,
all repeating the same weakness,
all in powerlessness compete.

Same thing last age. Federation.
Lost chance. Now all we hold as one
is sea, cricket, reggae, kaiso, sun.
What we deny: the history we own.'

The priest touched her hand. Then she grew
calm. His collar shone like an
angel's halo. 'Confession,
Father. Just for me and you.'

The heart's turning. Cry of the homesick.
Regret, guilt, a desire to go home.
Few, though, ever did return
for good. Seething sadly in the grip

of exile was better than the maw
of lack: Kingston, Georgetown – all over.
Most only returned as guests. After
taking some sun, soon time to withdraw.

Why had she exposed herself here?
The club a rutted, shallow niche
she'd always abhorred. Loneliness,
plain and simple, had brought her.

Outside, rescued by the privacy
of the car, the loud venting of tears;
What would she lose if she stayed here?
Could she find home in this country?

She passed Peachtree's High Museum.
Went in on a whim. Saw realist
workers' oily sweat, the subtlest
landscapes, Delaney's anthems

in yellow. It was seeing them
that lurched her mind to palm-fringed shores,
to hear the conch shells' song, surf's roar,
coral's hiss. How deny this poem?

CHAPTER TWENTY-FIVE

1.
So, next summer, trailing the migrant
voice, she touched the curdling surf
at bright Brandon, drunk with rising mirth,
until, laughing, she held its fragrance

raw. Something as urgent as waves
had swept her to these dear shores,
something strangely erogenous.
Her senses clung tight to the staves

of surf music, the throb of phallic
guitar on Brandon's long brown sand,
something speaking through the sound
that words can't trap, that, foaming, licks

at what's felt but can't be expressed.
But something crucial is being
revisioned here, something is healing
the deep pain so long repressed.

2.
She spies another loner on
the beach, senses some need in him
that echoes hers – in the taut limbs,
that absence of relaxation

in his dives to the sea's green depth,
boring like a glinting silver fish,
the look of effort on his face
as he surfaces, out of breath.

She knows he's been watching too,
conscious that her breasts like bobbing
buoys have caught his often glancing
eyes, notes how stealthily the good few

yards that distanced them have shrunk.
Well, why not? As the sea's scent assails
her – raw, amniotic – she hails
him boldly, almost a little drunk

in the surf-sprayed air. She sees him
wave and begin moving towards
her. She turns, then swishes shoreward,
though giving him a friendly grin.

Then gazing at something further on,
pursed lips seeming to frame a whistle,
she gathers bag and wraps a towel
round her waist. Then she puts on

sun glasses, straw hat, waves a hand
and heads down-beach, knowing he will
just stand there and watch her until
she's a dot on the distant sand.

CHAPTER TWENTY-SIX

1.
'When I see you now, you're my brightness.
When I need you now, you're my rightness.
You're my strength, the rock that anchors me.
I know your name; for me so holy.

And if I should again lose my way,
I know where to come, I know where to stay.
How can I forget the sunlight in your hair.
Your clear waters surround me.

And I, I love you so. I appreciate you
for touching my life the way that you do.
Where ever I go, I'm sure to come back again
to find myself in the place you live in.

When I see you now, you're my brightness.
When I need you now, you're my rightness.
You're my strength, the rock that anchors me.
I know your name; for me it's holy.'

Livvy was singing as he reached
the shore. Then eager sun-glazed eyes look
for her, but see only the grey smoke
that rises in slim spirals from each

distant rum refinery tower.
He tosses himself, face-down, like a man
starting push-ups, curls one bent arm
to support his head, looks for her

again; sees only the empty beach.
The sun blazes, a constant slow hand
deep-massaging his brown skin.
He dozes. Creeping, salty waves reach

and splash over him. Jumping up,
he strolls down-beach, pausing to stare
at curious stones mottling the shore,
just finding ways to fill time up.

At last, he spots something moving,
a blurred shape becomes an island,
grows distinct. At last! The woman
who'd hailed him from the wave. Searching

eyes narrow the space. No one stops
until they're standing face to face,
speechless like runners from a race.
Not seeing how the sand there drops

away (his gaze's on her) he stumbles,
startling an angry scuttling crab.
Seeing him about to fall, she grabs
his hand, and laughing they tumble

to the bed of Brandon's soft sand,
bathed in light streaming on the shore.
Now blessed by coral's hissing cure
they lie together hand in hand.

He the tuk, and she the ruk,
like curling anemones they dance
on the reef's floor. Like fish, entranced,
each caresses the other's rock

of pain, calcified knots of grief
long built, each touch a symbiotic
exchange, like the sinking love gift
of coralline algae to the reef.

Shot from petrified branches,
each ramiferous tentacle's
an interlacing potent cell,
numinous harmony of sexes.

All over coral tree, traces
of love, death, a rich complex fabric
of two weaving quilting architects:
bone upon bone of former races.

So, she was he and he was she,
eyes now filled with mutual longing,
they swim with white and yellow markings
atop Coral Crab's smooth bright belly;

atop long-spined arrowed Black Urchin
and his partner in terror, known as
Fireworm, poised to release rows
of white bristles into any skin;

atop parasitic surly red-
and-white striped banded Coral Shrimp;
atop Spiny Lobster who is limp
with rage at the strangers in his bed;

atop receptacle of basket sponge,
avoiding Touch-Me-Not; Fire Coral's red
glare; tube, brush sponges; Loggerhead,
fixed, mulish... (It's not his lounge!);

atop small-mouthed Grunts sharpening
their teeth; Snapper jaws chomping through
the ripples; rising, butterfly swarms
of Blue Angels; rainbow Parrot fish;

yellow Goat Fish... Great Barracuda,
solo, sliding in steely grey; Moray
eel bopping in olive dreads this way.
If Queen Conch and Helmet now could

announce all the rare beauty here,
what eloquence! See that stony
dead-living tree clothed in thick algae?
A Scorpion fish revealed by its stare.

2.
Here Creole voices, black and white,
and all else in between, in plural
patchwork bless with carnival,
each one same but yet unique.

Here the chance for true passion
where reefs, coralling, recreate,
unlike dream's united state,
fabled illusion, where metaphor is con.

Who wants hurtling leaps through time?
The blindfold that vision denies?
Who wants a life fashioned from lies,
that fears hearing, alone, it's own rhyme.

Here within carnival's bright inn,
the rising forest of the sea,
emblem of living-dead ecology,
heart wounds would heal when

rinsed with salt; and weary, footsore
wanderers find bright morning's grace
in sight of pink crab's scuttling race
on edenic casuarina shore.

3.
What providential lace-like touch
led them both searching to this beach,
without expectations, so that each
simply heeded the soft lurch

of sand, the cresting all-consuming surf,
the swift egrets' gentle clasp of wings
when, dauntless, they settle with songs
of great journeys, turmoils, deaths and births?

You ask, 'Did they exchange their names?
Did she say Levinia?
Did he whisper on that sand,
'Call me Tamer of the Seas'?'

No, they made exits, tittering,
'O I'm sorry.'
                    'O please excuse me.'
The moment had been an eternity,
a deep ancient song of possessing

glimpsed certainties, the chance
of pure congruence, yet, for all
they had common, both saw the wall
of self falling like a dying dance

or sandboxes' leaves falling on sand.
These hard symbols mirrored their ruins,
their grim histories, a truth that hymns
every living woman, living man.

NOTES

PART ONE

Chapter 1

Ichirouga: the Amerindian name for Barbados was Ichirouganaim.

bohio: the dwelling huts of the Tainos.

The Dragon's Mouth: a narrow sea channel of swift flowing water and cross currents on the north end of Venezuela which acts as a funnel to the Caribbean Sea and Trinidad.

machineel: a tree found along many Barbadian beaches, with poisonous fruit and a sap from the leaves that can cause severe blistering.

Shroud, Laycock, Jones, Chandler: all Barbados bays. Shroud is called Shroud Point.

Mapp's Cave, *Three Houses, Luke*: all sites of Arawak settlement in Barbados.

Chapter 2

Powell: English Captain, John Powell who in 1625 landed on Barbados and claimed the island for King James I of England. In 1627, his brother, Captain Henry Powell, established a colony at Holetown.

The Courteen Boys: Sir Peter and Sir William Courteen. The latter's finance syndicate was Barbados' first colonizing agency.

Carlisle: James Hay, first Earl of Carlisle was granted letters patent for Barbados' colonisation in 1628.

Downing: colonist George Downing.

Modyford: colonist Thomas Modyford who arrived on the island in 1647.

Drax: colonist James Drax, who arrived in 1620 and made his fortune by the 1650s.

Roundheads: Barbadian planters took a Royalist (Cavalier) stance which scorned the British Parliamentary (Roundhead) government. The planters, ostracized, finally gave in to what is called The Charter of Barbados in 1652, though on terms favourable to themselves.

Slave codes: first introduced in Barbados in 1661, and then made progressively more savage.

Cisterns raised: a method planters used for restraining blacks who came too close to their houses. The cisterns could be filled with hot water to throw on the slaves' bodies.

Sable Susannahs: References the Agustino Brunias painting of West Indian washerwomen circa 1770.

Cuffee: recorded as the mastermind of the 1675 revolt, probably of Akan origin, who was to have been crowned king. There are no records of his execution.

Anna Fortuna: slave snitch of the 1675 revolt.

Bulging eyes and the twisted mouth: references a line from the poem, "Strange Fruit," written in 1937 by the New York Jewish school teacher and political activist, Abel Meeropol (under the pseudonym Lewis Allan) and recorded by singer Billie Holiday in 1939.

The island weak from war./A restless slave: British-French war (1689-1713) which framed the 1692 revolt. Sampson, Hammon and Ben were all executed, along with 92 other men for their part in the revolt.

Chapter 3

Joshua Steele: a prominent planter who tried to introduce plans to rehabilitate the poor whites in the 1780s.

John Poyer: a white Creole historian whose *The History of Barbados* appeared in 1808.

Bussa: African-born leader of the 1816 slave rebellion, the largest in Barbados in which over 1000 slaves died in battle or were executed. All the reports of the rebellion attest to the sophisticated military planning of the slaves, suppressed only by superior British fire-power.

Chapter 4

Nanny: Nanny Grig or Grigg, a literate slave woman on Simmon's plantation.

Toussaint L'Overture: leader of Haiti's successful slave rebellion which resulted in the slaves declaring their independence from France in 1804.

after Trafalgar, Nelson's death: The Battle of Trafalgar was won by the British in 1805, giving them monopoly over the Atlantic. Their hero, Admiral Horatio Nelson, was mortally wounded in the battle.

Chapter 5

the Trade: the slave trade, abolished by the 1807 Act.

burn the canes: it was estimated that the planters lost some 175,000 pounds as a result of these fires.

Chapter 6

Big carnelian stars, are passed...: Bussa is given a burial normally reserved for members of the slave society of high status, such as healers/ diviners. Bussa can be seen as a type of diviner in that, as a leader of the 1816 revolt, he sought to avenge the wrongs done to his people and protect them from the "sickness" of slavery. The beads originating in Cambay, India, made their way through trade routes over the Red Sea to the east coast of Africa, and then, through overland Sahara and Sahel trade, to West Africa.

PART TWO

Chapter Seven

Ham's curse: Noah's curse on his son, Ham, for witnessing his drunken nakedness. In 18th century racist discourse Africans (Hamites) were seen as descendants of Ham, and the curse seen as a justification of slavery.

...to force an Act: the Public health Act of 1851.

Five days continuous labour...: a reference to stipulations in the 1840 Contract Law designed to curb labour mobility.

Chattels: tastefully painted chattel houses have ironically become part of the Barbados tourist heritage industry; their origins in planter denial of the ex-slaves access to freehold land is rarely mentioned.

circled by death... the occasional planter: In 1821, Reynold Alleyne Elcock, owner of the 620-acre Mount Wilton estate in St. Thomas, willed property to his ex-slaves for their protection of him and his family during the 1816 Bussa Rebellion. They had to wait until 1838 to benefit from the will.

Each cheque paid...: the slaves were given cheques of 85 pounds each with which to purchase lots.

Rock Hall: the first free village (inland from Holetown on the west, Caribbean sea, coast), established as a result of Elcock's bequest.

Chapter Eight

his liberal leaves...: Samuel Jackman Prescod (1806-1871) edited a newspaper called *The Liberal* which addressed issues of importance to the working class.

through legal means...: Prescod was the first known person of Black ancestry to sit in the House of Assembly.

Glenelg: Lord Glenelg of the Colonial Office.

MacGregor: Governor MacGregor (1836-1841).

Prescod didn't get to see full franchise: Prescod died in 1871.

BDA: The Barbados Defence Association was supported by Whites and the Black and Coloured middle-class.

Crown Colony/Government: civil policies legislated by the Mother Country, England, with the supposed purpose of seeking fair-play for all citizens.

Hennessey: Governor Hennessey (1834-1891) was governor between 1875-76.

Clenched stones ... drawn, glinting weapons...: a reference to the 1876 mass uprising, known as the Confederacy Riots.

The caveat Act...: the 1878 Education Act.

The caveat Report...: the 1896 Bree Commission Report that requested mandatory education for peasant-class children under the age of twelve.

The caveat hurricane...: the 1898 hurricane.

The Pylades: The H.M.S. Pylades, the vessel on which King Jaja (1821-1891) arrived in Barbados in 1891. He had previously been exiled to St. Vincent in 1888. The fullest account of King Jaja's life is to be found in S.J.S Cookey's *King Jaja of the Niger Delta: His Life and Times 1821 - 1891* (Nigeria 2005).

"King Jaja won' leh Becka 'lone,": the author deliberately presents this traditional Barbadian folk song as sung in its entirety by Becka. In the earlier rendition, lines 1 and 2 of each verse are sung by the female and line 3 and 4 by the male, in call-response.

195

Johnson: Harry H. Johnson; first, a British vice-consul, then consul to the Niger region.

Salisbury: Lord Salisbury: British Foreign Secretary.

Goshawk: H.M.S. Goshawk.

Patience: Jaja's newest intended wife. He was sent into exile before the marriage actually took place. **Authors's note**: *In recounting his story to Becka, Jaja refers to Patience as a friend and not as one of his wives, perhaps to avoid any religious conflict with the Christian Becka.*

Governor Sendall: Governor between 1889-91

Tenerife: Jaja died at the Camacho Hotel in Santa Cruz, Tenerife, the largest of the Canary islands, on July 7, 1891, at 6.00 a.m. He was some 60 miles from the coast of North West Africa.

Chapter Nine

men like Lofty and the Lynches: H.W. Lofty, merchant-politician. James A. Lynch and his son James Challenor Lynch.

The Canal: in 1904, the U.S. renewed construction of the Panama Canal.

Rawle, Clennel, and Charles: Rawle Parkinson, late 19th century head teacher of Wesley Hall School; Clennel Wickham, Editor of the *Barbados Herald*, the first Barbadian newspaper to represent working class views; Charles Duncan O'Neal (1879-1936), labour leader.

the Great War...: World War 1 (1914-1918).

The Ship: the chattel meeting house of the friendly societies known as Landships. They flourished in the 1920s, coming together in 1933 as the Barbados Landship Association.

Garvey's ways: Marcus Josiah Garvey, the Jamaican-born political activist who advocated repatriation of Blacks back to Africa and political action as a way to achieve social and economic rights.

a labour union: The Barbados Labour Union, formed in 1919.

a democratic league: The Democratic League, Barbados' first native political party, formed in 1924.

a working men's association: The Barbados Working Men's Association, formed in 1926.

Chapter Ten

I: the ghostly, invented voice of Sir Grantley Adams (1898-1971).

I'd watch this Clement closely.... Clement Payne (1904-1941), leader of Barbados' 1937 labour rebellion. He was born in Trinidad of Barbadian parentage.

U.N.I.A.: Universal Negro Improvement Association formed by Marcus Garvey.

N.W.C.S.A.: Negro Welfare Cultural and Social Association, a militant working-class movement in Trinidad.

The Commission: The Deane Commission, established by the Governor to investigate the origins and causes of the 1937 riots.

Mutual: The Barbados Mutual Life Assurance Society, formed in 1840. It was a dominant influence in Barbadian commerce.

The Square: Trafalgar Square in Bridgetown.

Governor Young: Governor Mark Young (1933-38).

Ormsby-Gore: The British Colonial Secretary.

Chapter Eleven

I joined with others...: the Barbados Labour Party (BLP) was formed in October 1938. Later, it was called the Barbados Progressive League before resorting back to its first name.

Seale: the radical Garveyite, Herbert Seale.

Lord Moyne: On January 14, 1939, Lord Moyne of the Royal Commission arrived in Barbados to investigate social and economic conditions in the West Indies.

build a structure, a future base: Trade Union Acts were passed after Lord Moyne's visit, one in 1939; another in 1940.

The Union: The Barbados Workers Union, formed on October 4, 1941.

Full franchise: Barbadians received full franchise to vote in 1950.

Full Cabinet government: this was achieved in 1958.

Walcott... turned on me: the late Sir Frank Walcott, the first General Secretary of the Barbados Workers Union. In 1954, Grantley Adams did not appoint Frank Walcott to a parliamentary post in the belief that his strength lay as a labour union organizer. It is alleged that this put a rift between the two men.

Errol... left me to go: Errol Barrow (1920-1987) was one of the radicals to leave the BLP to form the Democratic Labour Party (DLP) on April 27, 1955.

The Federation: the proposed Federation of the British West Indies. The idea was first introduced in 1932 in Dominica. The plans for Federation ended when Bustamante defeated Norman Manley in the Jamaican referendum of 1961 and then Eric Williams took Trinidad out of the Federation in 1962 ('one from ten leaves nought'.)

Bustamante: the late Sir Alexander Bustamante, Jamaican politician.

Manley: the late Norman Manley who, between 1955-1962, was Jamaica's chief minister.

Won... by a landslide: On December 6, 1961, the DLP won Barbados' national elections and Errol Barrow became the island's first Premier. Barrow's political success, followed on May 31, 1962, by the constitutional dissolution of the West Indies Federation, began the end of the Grantley Adams' political career.

I felt abandoned as the railway lines...: Barbados' railway service ended in 1934.

Cipriani: Michael Cipriani (d. 1945) founder of Trinidad and Tobago's first trade union.

Chapter Twelve

I: Errol Walton Barrow was the first Prime Minister of independent Barbados and revered as the father of the nation. He was the son of Rev. Reginald Grant Barrow and Ruth (née O'Neal), the sister of Charles Duncan O'Neal, founder of the Democratic League.

Once I dreamt: The admiral in the dream is British General, Sir George Ayescue, who bombarded the township of Oistins after the General Assembly of the island, resisting Crown Colony government, declared themselves an independent nation. After two days fighting, the 1651 Charter of Barbados treaty was signed at the Mermaid tavern in Oistins. In this treaty, the Barbadians agreed to pay four-and-a-half percent levies in exchange for the repeal of the Navigation Laws. Barbados' relationship to the British government was therefore established on the basis of contract and not of Crown Colony status.

Lee: the outgoing British Colonial Secretary, Fred Lee.

The Supremes: Diana Ross and the Supremes, at the height of their fame, gave a performance in Bridgetown as part of Barbados' Independence celebrations in November 1966.

The Garrison: the Garrison Savannah, used mainly for horse-racing, was the venue for Barbados' formal Independence ceremony.

Lesley: daughter of the late Errol Barrow.

Chapter Thirteen

The Farm: Culloden Farm, Prime Minister Errol Barrow's official residence.

The Community College: established in 1969.

the Black power revolt: In February 1970, a revolt took place in Trinidad involving workers, students and sections of the army. Although not part of the revolt, the American-based Stokely Carmichael (actually born in Trinidad) was one among many of the intellectual inspirations of the uprising. Carmichael visited Guyana where his Afro-centric rhetoric was seen in some quarters as insensitive to African-Indian relations. He was refused permission to stopover in Trinidad and the Barrow government passed the Public Order Act which made it possible to prevent Carmichael from visiting Barbados.

Grantley died: Sir Grantley Adams died in 1971.

Tom: son of Sir Grantley Adams and leader of the Barbados Labour Party.

Dipper: Dipper or the Skipper were Barrow's popular names.

King Dyal: a colourful character famed for his suits and support of English cricket teams at Kensington Oval (now deceased).

...the sound of Shilling's/guitar...: Barbadian strolling minstrel Shillingford Seymour Agard (1904-1982) whose busking was a feature of the city of Bridgetown from pre World War II until his death.

The day after our loss: The Democratic Labour Party lost the 1976 elections after 15 years in power.

a moses: a small Barbadian fishing boat.

"Kampala": the name of Errol Barrow's home near Paradise Beach.

Chapter Fourteen

Chaired/a meeting in Havana: Barrow chaired a meeting of Latin American and Caribbean countries in Havana at Fidel Castro's invitation.

Built an auditorium: The George Street Auditorium in Barbados.

Five local elections: Barrow ran, for his DLP party, three by-elections and two General Elections while in Opposition after 1976.

Kept Duffus at bay: Sir Hubert Duffus headed a Barbados Labour Party-appointed commission alleging corruption by Barrow while he was Prime Minister. Barrow was accused of amnesia for not being able remember detail of some of the events he was questioned about. No guilt was proven.

Rickey Singh: Already persona-non-grata in his native Guyana (the PNC Government nationalised his newspaper), Rickey Singh was the editor of the radical *Caribbean Contact*, the newspaper published by the Caribbean Council of Churches. He was also expelled from Grenada for opposing the American invasion.

George Lamming: Barbadian novelist known for his Marxist views.

Gabby: Anthony "Mighty Gabby" Carter, Barbados' most famous calypsonian.

When Tom died: Tom Adams, then Prime Minister, mysteriously died in 1985. Much speculation has been made of how he died. There was no official autopsy performed on his body.

sprats: small reef-dwelling fish.

The Auditorium: a reference to The Frank Collymore Hall situated in the Central Bank complex.

a local poet called Kellman: the poem quoted is from the collection, *The Long Gap* (Leeds: Peepal Tree Press, 1996)

Williams' words ringing in me: this is a quotation from a speech by the late Trinidad and Tobago Prime Minister, Sir Eric Williams, entitled 'From Slavery to Chaguaramas'.

Readers interested in further exploring the history of Barbados cannot do better than begin with Hilary Beckles' *A History of Barbados - From Amerindian Settlement to Nation-State.*

PART THREE

Chapter Fifteen

Brandon: Brandon's beach on the west coast, on the outskirts of Bridgetown

he would have battled till his strength...: he was caught in a whirlpool where two tides meet.

May pole: a species of the agave plant.

Black-belly sheep: a breed unique to Barbados and claimed to have African ancestry.

zygomatic: having an yoke or cross-bar shape.

Westbury: Westbury Cemetery in Bridgetown.

Chapter Nineteen

jumbie mushrooms: known as jumbie umbrellas, fungi associated with death.

Sharon's: Sharon's Moravian Church in St. Thomas.

Tuk... Ring Bang: Tuk or Ruk-a-Tuk are the original folk rhythms, Ring Bang, associated with Eddy Grant, a modern electrified derivation from those rhythms.

Chapter Twenty-One

Cave Hill: the University of West Indies campus in Barbados.

dougla: Trinidadian term for people of mixed African-Indian parentage.

Chapter Twenty-Two

King... Auburn's: Martin Luther King grew up in the Auburn neighbourhood of Atlanta.

chutney: the fast, modernised rhythms of Indo-Trinidadian music, based on women's wedding songs.

Peachtree's Kaya: an actual club in Atlanta, well-rated for its rave scene.

Chapter Twenty-Three

Fort Gordon: a 55000 acre Army base, with almost 20,000 employees.

Milosevic's cruelty: Slobodan Milosevic, the late President of Serbia and architect of the programme of ethnic cleaning that convulsed the former Yugoslavia in the 1990s. He died while under trial at the Hague in 2006.

Disgusta: Nickname for Augusta, Georgia. In part referring to the sulphur-like odour that persists in the air throughout the city, especially on a warm and/or humid day, but also as a place allegedly lacking any culture or refinement; a place of racism.

regain city too busy for race: Atlanta has been dubbed "the city too busy to hate."

Chapter Twenty-Four

U-Hauled: a brand of self-hired removal trucks in the USA.

a scuffle ... islands: A nod to Gordon Rohlehr's *A Scuffling of Islands: Essays on Calypso.*

Delaney's anthems in yellow: Beauford Delany, African-American painter (1907-1979). Delany once remarked, "I'm not interested in where people are descended from. I'm interested in where people are ascending to."

Chapter Twenty-Six

He, she tuk, and she, he ruk: word plays on ruk-a-tuk, the style of Barbados' indigenous Tuk music.

coralline algae: the red algae crucial in the ecology of the coral reef.

Fireworm: the bearded fireworm whose bristles when touched can flare out to give a swimmer painful irritation.

Loggerhead: loggerhead turtle.

Grunts: The white grunt, a fish which audibly grunts.

Queen Conch: The largest of Caribbean conches (strombus gigas).

Helmet: Helmet Shell (Cassis tuberosa), a large shellfish.

Scorpion fish: a spiny fish adept at disguise.

casuarina: a shore-growing, shrubby flowering tree, omnipresent in Barbados.

ABOUT THE AUTHOR

Anthony Kellman was born in Barbados in 1955, educated at Combermere School, at UWI (Cave Hill) and in the U.S. At eighteen he left for Britain where he worked as a troubadour playing pop and West Indian folk music on the pub and folk club circuit. During the 1980s he returned to Barbados where he worked as a newspaper reporter, then did a BA in English and History. Afterwards he worked in PR for the Central Bank of Barbados, experiences which he drew on in writing *The Coral Rooms*.

At this time he published two poetry chapbooks, *In Depths of Burning Lights* (1982) and *The Broken Sun* (1984), which drew praise from Kamau Brathwaite, among others.

In 1987 he left Barbados for the USA where he studied for a Masters of Fine Arts degree in Creative Writing at Lousiana State University. After completing in 1989 he moved to Augusta State University, Georgia, where he is a professor of English and creative writing.

In 1990 Peepal Tree published his third book of poetry, *Watercourse*, (which appeared with a glowing endorsement from Edouard Glissant), the novel, *The Coral Rooms* (1994), *The Long Gap* (1996) and *Wings of a Stranger* (2000). All his work has a powerful involvement with landscape, both as a living entity shaping peoples' lives and as a source of metaphor for inner processes. The limestone caves of Barbados have provided a particularly fertile source of inspiration.

In 2004 came his second novel, *The Houses of Alphonso*.

ALSO BY ANTHONY KELLMAN

The Coral Rooms
ISBN: 9780948833533   102pp   £6.95

Percival Veer has risen to the tenth floor of the Federal Bank of Charouga, has acquired a large and imposing house and a young and attentive wife. But satisfaction eludes him. Guilt over a past wrong begins to trouble him and a recurrent dream of caves disturbs his sleep. As Percy's inner world crumbles, he is gripped by an obsessive desire to explore the deep limestone caves of his island, dimly remembered from his boyhood. This gripping, poetic novel charts Percy's meeting with his spiritual guide, Cane Arrow, and his hallucinatory descent into the cave's depths.

Percival Veer's journey through the caves is not only a journey to truths that lie within him, but a journey to a vision of 'Creole magic': 'worlds of possibilities, coalescing visions and revisions of races and their juxtapositions.' This vision contrasts sharply with the cynical and pragmatic world of ethnic politics which has been his corrupting environment as a career bureaucrat.

'Realistic and dreamlike, explicit and mysterious... The descriptions are evocative & sensual. A compelling read.'
- Carole Klein.
'A realistic and convincing portrait of self-loathing'
- Wilson Harris.

The Houses of Alphonso
ISBN: 9781900715829 192pp £8.99

Barbadian-born Alphonso Hutson has lived in the USA for nearly sixteen years. But he cannot settle. He has dragged his long-suffering American wife, Simone, and their children from house to rented house. He has refused to share with her any real explanation for the complex feelings that drive him. But this time she has had enough of his 'sorry restlessness', refuses to move with him and threatens the end of their marriage. Only then is Alphonso forced into confronting the ghosts that propel his perpetual migrancy.

The ghosts lie in his native Barbados. There is the love, shame and guilt he feels for the dead parents whose funerals he failed to attend, and there is the mystery of the brother he has never seen, hidden away in an institution. All is complicated by his mixed feelings for his homeland. It is the place that still feeds his imagination, but as a boy from a Black working class family he has felt excluded from the class structures of a country still dominated by a privileged White minority.

There is also the family house, locked up and at risk of being vandalised and Alphonso finally recognises that he cannot put off making a return, the first since his departure. In what follows Kellman combines a poetic and imaginative exploration of Alphonso's personal journey into his past, with an acute engagement with racial and political issues as he rediscovers his country in the midst of turmoil as the old order is challenged.

Watercourse
ISBN: 9780948833373   64pp   £5.99

The celebrated Martiniquan poet and novelist Edouard Glissant writes: '*Watercourse* is more than a collection of poems. It is the continual amazement evoked by Caribbean landscape: a single dialogue between the sea and the land... a song whose dazzling waves foam among the islands... Anthony Kellman's poetry has the strength and sweetness of vegetation with the power of progressively revealing to us the nature of the earth in which it grows.'

Joseph Bruchac writes: 'His enchantment is that dangerous, double-edged power of a Prospero, a magician who has visioned life in all its complexity...'

The Long Gap
ISBN: 9780948833786   64pp   £6.99

The Long Gap is a passionate exploration of the Caribbean exile's need 'to go back/to clutch the roots of the word'. Writing out of the the fear of the 'gap' which can grow too long, Kellman engages with his Barbadian heritage as one which both sustains and drives to anger. In language which echoes the rhythms of the 'tuk' band and the 'scat of the guitar strum', he celebrates the traditions of resistance and creative invention, but excoriates the islands of cocaine, political corruption and subservience to external masters.

Bruce King writes: 'Tony Kellman is always trying something different... He is a serious poet and the various contradictions and affiliations found in his verse embody those of the Caribbean and, to generalise, most poetry. A formalist attracted towards, oral, folk and popular traditions, he also mixes the highly lyrical with dialect and the prose-like. I especially like his metaphors and patterns of sound. When reading these poems you feel that... here is one of our best younger poets.'

Wings of a Stranger
ISBN: 9781900715447   71pp   £7.99

In the continuing rite of return to his native Barbados from longer and longer away, something has happened for Tony Kellman. No longer are these the alienated poems of *the long gap*, of belonging nowhere. With greater establishment in America has come, *on the wings of a stranger*, the capacity to embrace this past and to see wholly afresh what was once familiar and unremarked. Parallel to these poems of place, are those that explore new love and its power to heal.

As well as Barbados, there are poems set in worlds as different as sharecropping Georgia and Yorkshire, England. In all of them one hears Kellman's signal voice which combines his urbane capacity to 'hum forever simple pleasure' and the ecstatic vision of a poet who 'puts on the garment of praise' to 'retell our special story'.

NEW FROM PEEPAL TREE

Laurence A. Breiner
Black Yeats: Eric Roach and the Politics of Caribbean Poetry
ISBN: 9781845230470; pp. 302; £17.99

For readers of West Indian literature, a study of Eric Roach requires
no justification. He is the most significant poet in the English-
speaking Caribbean between Claude McKay (who spent nearly all of
his life abroad) and Derek Walcott. Roach began publishing in the
late 1930s and continued, with a few interruptions, until 1974, the
year of his suicide. His career thus spans an extraordinary period of
Anglophone Caribbean history, from the era of violent strikes that
led to the formation of most of the region's political parties, through
the process of decolonization, the founding and subsequent failure
of the Federation of the West Indies (1958-1962), and the coming
of Independence in the 1960s. This book presents a critical analysis
of all of Roach's published poetry, but it presents that interpretation
as part of a broader study of the relations between his poetic activity,
the political events he experienced (especially West Indian Federa-
tion, Independence, the Black Power movement, the 'February
Revolution' of 1970 Trinidad), and the seminal debates about art
and culture in which he participated.
By exploring Roach's work within its conditions, this book aims
above all to confirm Roach's rightful place among West Indian and
metropolitan poets of comparable gifts and accomplishments.
Laurence Breiner is the author of the critically acclaimed *Introduction
to West Indian Poetry*.

Stewart Brown
Tourist, Traveller, Troublemaker: Essays on Poetry
ISBN: 9781845230531; pp. 320; £14.99

Major essays on the work of Caribbean and African poetry, including
Kamau Brathwaite, Frank Collymore, Olive Senior, Kwame Dawes,
James Berry, Linton Kwesi Johnson, Niyi Osundare, Femi Oyebode,
Jack Mapanje and others. With the subtext of a mistrust of postcolonial
theory and its whole academic industry, Stewart Brown, as a practicing
poet, both establishes the autobiographical grounds from which the
essays are written and asserts that the poetry is more important than
its criticism. This is a collection that is wide-ranging, provocative,
intellectually rigorous – and eminently readable.